Published in the United States of America by
The Guild for Psychological Studies Publishing House
2230 Divisadero Street
San Francisco, California 94115

Cover Art: Susan Renfrew
Cover Design: Dorothy Nissen
Typesetting and Layout: PAN Typesetters, Eugene, Oregon

Library of Congress Cataloging in Publication Data

Howes, Elizabeth Boyden, 1907
Intersection and Beyond.

Includes indexes.
1. Psychology and religion — Addresses, essays, lectures. 2. Psychoanalysis and religion — Addresses, essays, lectures. I. Title.
BF51.H64 1986 201'.9 86-3067
ISBN 0-917479-04-1 (pbk. : v.1)
ISBN 0-917479-07-6 (pbk. : v.2)

INTERSECTION AND BEYOND

Twelve lectures on the commingling
of religious values and the insights
of analytical psychology

by

Elizabeth Boyden Howes, Ph.D.

GUILD FOR PSYCHOLOGICAL STUDIES

GUILD FOR PSYCHOLOGICAL STUDIES
2230 Divisadero Street
San Francisco, CA 94115

For Ruth Warnick
(1906-1970)

the depth of whose
belief in this book
has enhanced its
meaning immeasurably —
with gratitude for this
and so much else.

TABLE OF CONTENTS

INTRODUCTION

In 1963 *Intersection*, containing seven lectures I had given over a period of several years, was published by the Guild for Psychological Studies. This was quite quickly sold out.

In 1968, that same edition was published in Zurich by Origo Verlag, under the title of *Die Evangelen im Aspekt der Tiefenpsychologie*, having been translated into German by Mrs. Kathrin Asper. This came about through the response of Dr. Carl Loosli of Geneva to this booklet.

Now, in 1971, a much revised and enlarged edition has been published by the Guild, containing six of the original lectures and six new ones. The new title, *Intersection and Beyond*, indicates changing and evolving concepts.

Certain fundamental things need to be stated here. All these articles were originally lectures given either under the Guild for Psychological Studies or for Analytical Psychology Clubs or in churches, and two were given in London for the Guild of Pastoral Psychology. Although some polishing has been done, essentially they have been allowed to stand in their original and more spontaneous form, with added material. Some were originally lectures and some were extemporaneous talks, transcribed and later revised. Because of the focus on core ideas, it is inevitable that a certain amount of overlapping will be found in some of the lectures, and no effort was made to edit this out.

Because they are spread over many years some of them are occasionally "dated" but still relevant — i.e. a reference to the assasination of John F. Kennedy as a happening that has just occurred remains as it is. The world has moved so fast that many references that were fresh at the moment of their telling are now taken for granted, yet have not necessarily lost their significance.

Throughout all the articles the *Records* refers to *The Records of the Life of Jesus*, edited by Dr. Henry B. Sharman. This book is the one used in the Guild seminars.

However, all quotations from the Gospels will give the biblical chapter and verse.

After much consideration the pronoun references to God are capitalized (i.e., as Him) used in the generic sense of including Him/Her.

In a very real sense this booklet stands as a basic expression for the Guild for Psychological Studies. Since the first issue of *Intersection* the Guild has expanded not only in its program of seminars, in the training of new leaders and therapists but also in carving out and clarifying a point of view which combines the rich insights of the Analytical Psychology of C. G. Jung, the contribution of Fritz Kunkel with the insights into the authentic meaning of the teachings of Jesus as discovered in study with Henry B. Sharman. For thirty years my own experience has been as an analyst in the Jungian tradition and a leader of seminars under the Guild.

My only hesitancy in issuing this booklet rested on the recognition that a good deal of development of concepts and experience has gone on since the earlier work, and for those interested in what is here, other writings are forthcoming.

In conclusion I wish to thank Dr. Sheila Moon for her constant help in clarifying what I really wanted to say. And special thanks to Miss Florence Little and Miss Diana Lusk for their devoted and time-consuming work on revision of the new edition.

Elizabeth B. Howes, Ph. D.

THE RELIGIOUS FUNCTION OF THE EGO

A statement of Mrs. Carl Jung has stayed in my mind since one of the last times I talked with her in 1955. She said, "There are egos, and egos, and egos, and the problem is to find the real one." This statement holds within it all the implications about the ego which I want to discuss. Three things are implicit in Mrs. Jung's words: that there is such a thing as a "not-real" or "false ego"; and that the "real ego", which in its most creative role is religious, can be discovered and transformed through work and sacrifice.

What is meant by ego? Let me give what I consider to be essentially a Jungian definition: The ego is the "I". It is what I know of myself, of my reactions and my attitudes. It is my conscious side. It is the center of what is me; it is the center of what responds to all that is "not me", which includes "you", the world, every situation, every phenomenon over which I do not have control. Different from the ego, whether real or false, is the non-ego. The non-ego includes all of the inner world of dynamisms and of those large patterns of reaction, the archetypes. It contains, in the words of Martin Buber, all the possible "thous" of the universe. The "I" (ego) is that which responds to the "thou" (non-ego), whether it is inside or outside. My cat or dog, objects, friends, social institutions, the reactions of others, the stars, the wind, the dream of last night, the reaction that came unbidden in a certain situation from another person - these are not "I." What I do with them, how I react to them, how I see them, how I look at them, how I feel consciously about them how I respond and act — these are "I". And the whole purpose of this paper is to try to indicate how the ego could meet each moment and respond to it, and why the ego fails to do so through becoming centered on itself (egocentric).

It would be well to point out that of course the term "ego" is not peculiar to Analytical Psychology. It is to be found in many academic sources, textbooks, and is used by many schools of thought. But the definition of "ego" in Analytical Psychology is unique, in the sense that it is the only one where the ego is seen as an expression of something deeper within the psyche, is conceived as an extension of the Self — the Self's thrust into consciousness. In fact, the real Self, the central archetype, can, I believe, only be fulfilled with the help of the ego.

The value of the ego will already be apparent. It has everything to do with how I live, whether I really "live" at all, how the span of my life is filled or left empty. It has everything to do with how I see reality. And there is added urgency today, because of the nature of world history, that "the doors of perception be cleansed" and that we see things as they are.

What is the function of the real ego — that which I will call the Creative "I"? Surely the "I" is not something to be eliminated. Rather it is something which is essential to the wholeness of personality. The Creative "I" responds — has responsibility, has the ability to respond both to inner world and outer world. In fact, it mediates between the two. The Creative "I" is the maker of choices. It faces the real facts of existence, it appraises what can and what cannot be changed, and its attitude is one of either acceptance or alteration. It is the judge and the discriminator of what are the possibilities within any given inner or outer situation. The Creative "I" must face and explore the inner world beyond itself and must relate to the outer world beyond itself. In both cases it must see the real inner and outer worlds not as narrow, limited, partial worlds, but as God's worlds; and it has the responsibility to face both these worlds, to relate to both, and somehow to bring them into some kind of cohesive whole. The Creative "I" works at freedom — freedom from those things which narrow life, and freedom for those things which enlarge life. Its purpose is not to manipulate but rather to "be" in its freedom. This is its essence.

Let me speak first, then, of the relationship of the Creative "I" to the inner world, then of its relationship to the outer world, and finally, of how it brings the two worlds together.

The relationship of the ego to the inner world is probably that which Analytical Psychology has dealt with most fully. Yet I would venture to say as a Jungian that perhaps one of the more legitimate criticisms of Analytical Psychology is that it often fails to emphasize the function of the ego in both aspects. It is too easy and attractive to get lost in the inner world — in the "museum of the archetypes", as one Jungian put it — and not really to relate creatively to outer realities. The Creative "I" needs to discriminate and to separate itself from the non-ego or, as Dr. Jung has called it, the objective psyche. The Creative "I" must respond and relate to what comes up in life situations as well as in dreams. It must have great openness and willingness to listen to all of the levels of the unconscious, and to all of the opposites, ambiguities, ambivalence, which speak out in manifest living. It takes a great deal of courage and humility on the part of the ego to face two ways, but only in so doing does one learn who one is and what one is all about. This is true freedom.

The ego relationship to the inner world is extremely interesting to observe in dreams, and this must be touched on briefly. The ego has two roles — one as a figure in the dream, and the other as an interpreter of the dream. Relative to the ego as dream figure, three questions could be asked about each dream. (1) Where is the ego in the dream and how is it relating to the other elements in the dream? (2) What kind of activity is going on in the dream in relation to the ego, and is it appropriate activity? Is it active enough or too active? Passive enough or too passive? Exactly what is the quality of its action? (3) Is the ego in the dream biased and defensive, identified and contaminated by archetypal material, or is it freely itself?

Let me give a few examples of the development of the ego in dreams. The first series is from a woman in her late 30's or early 40's. The first dream at the beginning of analysis was as follows. "I am by a pool, a young woman like myself jumps into the water and doesn't reappear. I do not jump in to rescue her." The second dream, considerably later: "I am in a hospital room but not sick. A woman figure (representing my most neurotic conflict) comes in quietly and with determination. She is about to take a pill, under doctor's orders, to die. It is a sober suicide, a voluntary, necessary act. I am horrified but have a tremendous sense of awe and do not move." The third dream, two years later: "I am by a pool. A father-spirit figure behind me moves gently aside to make way for a beautiful hermaphroditic figure, half human and half divine, to dive into the pool. There is a sense of purgation and cleansing." In all three dreams the ego (the dreamer) is passively alert, or positively inactive, yet there is a growing awareness of meaning. There is a creative non-interference. In the first example it was quite right that the dreamer did not jump in to save the girl — but it took a long time to see this. In the second dream, she had a deep sense of acceptance of the death of her own neurotic side, and this was a great advance. In the third, she felt it was right to be cooperative with the spirit side and to make way for the new figure in a definite movement of helpfulness.

The second series is from a woman patient somewhat older than the previous case. These dreams came quite close together in time:

> (1) A voice said, "Dig in your own neighborhood and you will find gold."
>
> (2) Two Arabians were making gold as a secret process, because people might steal it; I observed it and felt the batch might have to be thrown out because there was too much water.

In the first dream a voice was giving the ego a definite command, and it responded with no resistance. For the dreamer this was like a call to much more activity to counterbalance her passivity. In the second dream she felt definitely involved in a positive and deep process, in a cooperative, discriminating way.

Let me give as one final example the initial dream of a middleaged man:

> I am standing on the rim of a canyon with another man. We both see lots of dark-skinned people who are down on the canyon bottom as a

> result of their failings. They were so hopeless and dark. I spoke up and said they must be taken care of, must be brought back. The other man stayed aloof, as if scared to be involved.

Here the ego of the dreamer was definitely willing to confront the rejected side of the dreamer, but another part wanted nothing to do with the process. Two attitudes towards the inner world are clearly shown, and there seems to be an awareness of both, although not a resolution.

It is very fascinating to watch this role of the ego in the actual analytical process of the interpreting of dreams. The ego is, of course, involved also in interaction with the analyst, and in making judgments concerning choices of interpretation. It is really the ego in the deepest, richest sense that has to make judgments as to what is really felt, with fullest integrity, to be the right interpretation.

Now let me turn to the role of the ego in its approach to outer reality. It must be remembered that the ego becomes infinitely more sharply defined in its function in the objective world as it works with the subjective, and thus becomes free from identification with the inner processes. Thereby it is also free for creative use. As it grows in clarity it can be concerned constantly with the question of response and choice in every situation in which the person is confronted with a multiplicity of values and possibilities. The Creative "I" must learn to be, paradoxically, spontaneous in deliberate acts of discrimination. This is the essential moral quality of the ego. This means that the ego is involved in a very difficult ethical problem because it must decide whether it should be on the side of that which is unorthodox and unconventional, or on the side of the conventional and orthodox. This ego, if working and choosing and reacting out of the deeper complexity of the psyche, cannot choose in the automatic categories of "good and evil", "dark and light". It has to be sensitive and open to possibilities and potentialities, and often the *decision* has to be against everything which the ego had ever thought was "right".

Let us take the role of the ego in the outer world one step further, and see how it relates to the meaningfulness of events. Dr. Jung says, "Synchronicity takes the coincidence of events in time and space as meaning something more than mere chance, namely, a peculiar interdependence of objective events among themselves as well as with the subjective state of the observer. The attitude of the observer is central." This attitude, then, is the action of ego really being aware of the purposive and synchronous nature of all events, continually being concerned with Why. "Why did this person appear on my horizon?" "Why did this something happen today?" "Why have outer events shaped up as they have?" Here awareness means not seeing things as accidents but always asking about purposes and values.

Why is this not usually or easily achieved? Why does it not always happen? What are the obstacles to the ego's encompassing of purposes? Why does one have to work so hard in order to find this real ego whose function is to make a cohesive whole of the inner and outer?

Mythologically — and perhaps even theologically — some answers to these vital questions may be found in the Garden of Eden myth in Genesis, which seems to me to illustrate what I call God's freedom in man. In this myth the ambivalence of Yahweh is expressed in the fact that one commandment comes from him and an opposed one from the serpent whom he created. And man was confronted with the freedom of choice to relate or not to relate to supra-personal values. He had the awful (and awe-full) possibilities of going off on his own Luciferian way, or of responding to the individual and ultimate nature of reality. In this great paradigm is the challenge to man as to whether he is cursed, or blessed with responsibility.

Psychologically, in more personal and less cosmogonic terms, the ego and the egocentric images and defenses have been very provocatively considered in the writings of Fritz Kunkel, of certain neo-Freudians such as Karen Horney and Eric Fromm, and of the English Jungian, Dr. Culver

Barker. All these psychotherapists, in one way or another, have described similar ego development problems. In the early stages of childhood, they find, the ego has to be protected both inwardly and outwardly from the encroachment of its milieu. The childhood ego is sensitive, vulnerable, uncertain, and the powers threatening it are very great. It builds defenses — absolutely necessary defenses at that stage of childhood — and thereby it loses its own potential reality. It is so busy defending itself that it can not fulfill its function of establishing its own nature and true relatedness. As adults we find ourselves in the same situation, still letting these idealized images and egocentric patterns, which we had to have in our early years, limit our existence. They have been invaluable, and probably we would not have survived without them, but in our adulthood they must be "sacrificed" in order that the ego be fulfilled.

What are some of the major forms and patterns of the ego's unfulfillment? Although there are innumerable complexities, of course, I must here simplify the problem and discuss only three basic kinds of unfulfilled ego. The extreme form is where there is no ego structure to support personality, where consciousness is completely overcome by the unconscious. This engulfment by the unconscious powers is what characterizes borderline psychotic states, which are really not the concern of this paper. They are, of course, the most blatant and pathological sicknesses of the ego. Dr. Kunkel used to say, "These are the ones who have the frail canoes in a raging sea."

The second form is of more common occurrence and has to do with ways in which egocentric defenses, which make us self-centered instead of objective or value-centered, act to prevent relationship to the real Self. Such defenses make us see the world in limited partial terms, either through undermining us by self-negation, abasement and inferiority, or through putting us on the precarious perch of inflation and self-aggrandisement. To carry out Dr. Kunkel's picture, the self-negation defense resembles a fishing boat that won't let itself leave the dock, while the self-aggrandising defense is like an ocean liner on a duck-pond. In both cases there is archetypal involvement, usually of some aspect of the parental problem.

The more subtle third form in which the ego is unfulfilled has to do with its identification with outer, collective prestige and status, and/or with central religious concepts and archetypes. Some of the things which we fail to analyze enough are the cultural factors operative today. These go far, far deeper in our own psyches than we like to recognize. It is easy to talk about the pressure to conformity, the emphasis on the extrovert world in which we live, the power of authoritarianism, the Madison Avenue image. It is not easy to see, in concrete ways, how our own specific egos get involved with these images and elements inside us, and how the ego clings blindly to them. For example, it is not enough for a woman with a negative masculine pull to authority to understand how this pull operates; she must see all the tiny ways her insecurity actually makes her behave in everyday situations, actually catches her up in the cultural dominants. One can understand in general how in the man a negative feminine pull toward lethargy or inertia emasculates the ego. It is another thing to see concretely how this passitivity may make the man "sell out" on vital cultural issues where a masculine stand should be taken. I stress this because this kind of unconscious ego involvement, even on the part of analyzed people, is of social and historical importance. We need much more analysis of the dominant images of our world and how, actually and existentially, they catch us. It is disturbing to come upon people who have had lengthy analyses and yet who have not uncovered this level, people in whom the ego, for all its inner work, has not related inner images to society and so the individual is caught in prestige and power patterns, only under other guises than the ordinary ones. This is not true individuality.

One of the most subtle and dangerous aspects of this latter problem is the unconscious identification with various forms of the Christian archetype. This, of course, is a whole study by itself and became increasingly important in Dr. Jung's emphasis, and certainly in my own. We know the depth to which the ego can be caught in the one-sided, light, bright side of the Self, and the split and the guilt thereby produced in the psyche. We have not analyzed deeply enough this engulfment of the ego in its most hidden forms. Therefore we tend to avoid seeing this split and its potential redemption by turning to religious expression which tries to omit the ego altogether, or adopts a limited and circumscribed attitude to the ego. We in the West must include the ego in our religious expression, and the ego must include its relationship to the problem of the evil and darkness.

Let me cite a dream of a young woman who, after a long analysis, was at last at work at her own religious problem:

> Am on a bus with a group of people. The bus has stopped and a man gets on. He is wearing a cape and as he looks at me there is some kind of challenge in his appraisal. Then we are all in a community as a group and the people are losing their souls, or rather, their feelings. I watch them day by day as one after another begins to stare blankly into space and walk about like automatons. It seems that those who have lost their feelings are followers of the man on the bus and the camp has divided into two groups now — his followers and mine. I am desperately trying to save my people from this terrible fate and to rescue those in his camp who have lost their feelings. It seems there is some way to do this if I can only find it. It seems in some vague way that he wants me to find the way, too, even though he must oppose me. Then I am standing a little apart from my group near a doorway and I see a dove flying lazily above me. The bird circles around and slowly comes to rest on my hand. I think it is the most beautiful bird I have ever seen. It is pure white and has a most intelligent expression. 'You can save them now,' it says. 'Anyone you touch with your hand will be saved, or anyone who touches anything that your hand has touched, especially dirt.' I go

about touching people and see them beginning to get their feelings back and the expressions change — like mannequins coming to life they begin to move and go about their way with animation. I do not want the man to know that I have found a way to save the people yet, so I caution everyone to act just as though nothing has happened, for in this way I may save the man. They promise they will not let him know. Now there is open contest between the man and me. He comes to my camp to try to capture my people and they all mingle together. I sense that if I can get to the man and touch him they will all be saved. He tries to avoid me but finally I hurl myself at him, grasping his arm. He becomes quite still and slowly begins to change as though awakening from some bewitched sleep. 'I am so glad,' he says, 'that you found the way!' I look up and see the dove just over our heads, and as the bird looks at me I realize what and who it is.

What is the relationship of this woman's ego to her religious problem? In the dream words, she, the ego, is on the side of trying to save the people who are the real people (primarily people who have become so automatic as to be dead) from the domination of the Satanic figure of the man. Yet at the same time she knows from the very beginning that the Satanic figure has a very positive side. There is a deep awareness of this. Also she, the ego, has a clear relationship to the bird, which she associated with the bird of eros, bird of love. She said, "I realize what and who it is." It represented, she felt, spirit qualities between her and the man, so that when she finally hurled herself at him there could be a transformation. Such a dream clearly articulates both man's need for God and God's need for man. The dreamer, after a great deal of work on her part, now stands on the side of creativity and of rebirth.

How can this real ego be discovered? Dr. Gerhard Adler said, in a seminar, that the ego has to be born, and the ego has to be reborn. It is, I believe, born and reborn through the constant process of sacrifice. In fact the sacrificial motif seems to underlie the whole growth of the ego. First, there is the level of the willingness to sacrifice the egocentric patterns, the idealized images, the defenses. Then, after the establishment of the real ego which is secure and adapted, its dominion must be sacrificed to that of the deeper Self. As Eric Neumann pointed out, the dragon has constantly to be slain throughout life, but the form of the dragon changes. The real ego is continually born as one finds continually whatever is the appropriate action called for and responded to. The birth is constantly going on, at all levels, repetitively yet differently.

How can we know about and aid in this birth of the real ego in ourselves? What are the criteria by which we can know? How can we work at it? We must begin to be observant of our egocentricities and false patterns, must watch the sensitive points, the compulsive acts, must see how egocentric patterns manifest themselves in reactions to others. We must try to "see ourselves as others see us". Through these means we can begin to be free of our defensive systems.

There is also the matter of the ego working to free itself from the autonomous relationship to, or identity with, its unconscious side. This sort of autonomy is similar to egocentricity, but also very different. Several dreams will show the difference: A young man dreamed, "I was dying and feeling very dramatic. Then I was aware I wasn't going to, and suddenly I knew I wasn't Hamlet after all!" He saw this as describing his own self-pity and indecision, and realized with some humor that his ego was choosing to disidentify from this egocentric pattern. In the second instance, a man dreamed he was talking to friends about the war, and said, "I went through it with a poor-little-me attitude, and I am sick of it!" He recognized his own masochism and was trying to free himself from it. Both of these dreams are statements of ego beginning to separate from egocentricity.

At the second level of renunciation, when the ego must be modified to include the larger whole, the dream of a woman who thought of herself as "strong" is a dramatic example. She dreamed a voice said, "You didn't know how to read the tides." She took it that her ego was in danger of getting identified with her own too-strong side, and she had to be willing to let it go in order to move more with the feminine "moon rhythm" in the unconscious.

There are many ways to observe one's own ego and to bring into consciousness its struggle for growth. One very simple thing that is extremely helpful is to ask one's self questions. How many opportunities were there today where I had to make a decision? Was I really the chooser? How many times was my ego really driving me, instead of having something else direct it? Was I taken over by autonomous behavior instead of acting from my Self? How many times, inwardly or outwardly, was I pushed around instead of the "Creative I" making the choice? When was I present today? Was I ever present in any sense? Ever really there? Did I see any of the people that I talked to today? Did I see the sunset, the flowers? Did I see my animal? Such simple questions as these can be genuine aids in the knowing and being able to use the true ego. In "The Transformation Symbolism in the Mass", Dr. Jung wrote, "A sacrifice proves you possess yourself, for it does not mean just letting yourself be passively taken; it is a conscious and deliberate self-sacrifice which proves you have full control of yourself, that is, of your ego . . . the ego must make itself conscious of its claim and the Self must cause the ego to renounce it." What a supreme challenge it is for the ego, conscious of its claims, to be ready to sacrifice itself for the deeper aspect of the Self!

By now I hope it is apparent that the religious function of the ego is implicit. More explicity, the ego functions religiously when it takes on, as a very conscious act, dedication or commitment to supra-personal values—when it decides, in Jung's terms, with deliberation to go the way of wholeness. It has been my interest over many years to work not only as an analyst but also as a leader in seminars where I think this element is particularly stressed. Through my dual work I have come to make the distinction between a strong uncommitted ego and a weak but committed ego. I have a deep conviction that when with full consciousness we have really made such a dedication, it has a profound effect on our analytical journey, on the relation of the journey to lived life, and on the deeper bringing together of inner and outer values. A patient of mine, who had a fairly weak but very dedicated ego, dreamed that his decision about marriage must be in the context of the will of God. Such a dream would indicate an ego obviously related in a very purposive way to whatever the dreamer calls the "will of God", a will different than that which is in consciousness. When the conscious side takes on this more total attitude it is involved in what I would call the problem of the discipline of the ego, which certainly can be worked at in other ways than through analysis. (As an analyst, I obviously believe psychotherapy is the main way for many of us, but I do not believe that in itself analysis necessarily does the job.)

One of the religious functions of the ego is how it chooses to find time or "steal" time (for time always has to be "stolen") to work at transformation. One of the great needs in the field of psychology and religion is this experimenting with techniques, procedures, ways of meditation and prayer consistent with our analysis, because these are aspects of a necessary centralizing process. I would stress, as Jung did, that these must meet the needs of the Western psyche, not the Eastern. I myself have been experimenting with, and have led seminars in, introversion, meditation, and prayer in which Martin Buber's idea of dialogue was emphasized as an inner interaction. Here the "I" relates elements which must also be seen as "Thou". The dialogue between "I" and an unknown inner "Thou" is a certain form of active imagination, in which the way the ego talks and the parts reply helps us to deepened self-insight. I believe this idea of the dialogue of the ego and the parts has dynamic possibilities in it. Sometimes two or more elements in a dream can be brought into active interrelatedness. The dialogue should be entered into only after one evokes the central presence of God. This is a profound religious act, and is not done too easily nor too often; but it is a most creative combination of the human and the divine.

One of the reasons why I am so concerned with the Synoptic Gospels is that I believe that in the Gospels we have the living search; we are shown a man who exactly and completely lived the thing I have been talking about — the conscious relatedness to the divine. In his baptism, in his wilderness experience, in such profound parables as the story of the prodigal son, in his own living, in Gethsemane, Jesus continually confronts us with an extremely Creative "I". He lived in relationship to the very deepest forces within himself and in the Universe. If this be construed as "mysticism", let it be. It may even be related to the "mysticism" of which Dr. Jung has been accused. If so, this is mysticism involving individuality through relationship. This is not the mysticism of absorption, nor the "we-are-one", not identification. This is the mysticism of wholeness. It comes through relatedness, when the Creative "I" is present but is transformed through becoming voluntarily obedient to the divine.

Lastly, I would say that the Creative I accepts the limitations of finiteness in accepting death, acknowledges the reality within which it lives, and expresses the Infinite. It lives within its own limited finite world, and the acceptance of this is the greatest pain, to be sure, but without that pain the Creative I would not come into being and there would be no incarnation within anyone. I believe it is also true that the infinite could never be brought into finite manifestation if the I did not do so.

When the ego is fully dedicated and sensitive to what Charles Williams called "the Holy Thing," and to the possible birth of the Holy Thing, inwardly and outwardly, it is functioning religiously. And when the I is aware that this birth is both the object of its own work and the result of grace from the other side, even more is it functioning religiously. It is then creatively submissive to the Mystery, and the Mystery, by becoming manifest in the individual, is potentially manifest in the outer world and its history.

THE ETERNAL QUESTION
WHAT IS IT? WHO ASKS IT?

It would be very fascinating to begin this paper by asking you what you have projected into the title. What do you think is the Eternal Question? I hope you will write down in your own mind what your projection is into the title. Then check it, work with it and see how it fits or differs from what will be suggested later. It would also be fascinating to speculate on the first question that was ever asked by man. Once he had language, what was the first question man ever asked to another man, to himself, to his world or to his universe? You might also ask yourself what is the most important question that you have ever been asked in your whole life, and equally significant to ask yourself what is the most important question that you have ever asked of life itself. And lastly, it would be very meaningful to ask yourself what is the question that you would most dread being asked by either another person or by life itself.

What is questioning? Let us break down one of the most fundamental qualities or abilities that we take utterly for granted: the ability to ask questions, the ability to receive and respond to questions. The fact that questioning is there, and that from it dialogue becomes possible, is a manifestation of the ability of reflective thinking and of heightened consciousness. It produces perhaps the first step in our creative anxiety which is the goading process that leads to growth.

What is a question? A question is something asked, stated, put by someone to someone, or to something. It assumes two parties, the asker and the responder. It assumes that someone is listening. It is therefore a special form of dialogue as a dialectic process. There is a question as thesis, a response as antithesis, and a new insight as synthesis, for neither party, the questioner or the responder, stays exactly where he was after the question. A new point, what Fritz Kunkel called "the third point", always emerges. New facts are available from the questioning process, whether it is a question for information, a simple question of what time it is (if that is simple), or a question for insight, such as, "What do you think about this?" The insight can lead to a tremendous sense of on-goingness and impetus for living. The quesion-response configuration, the interaction involved, assumes that new truth or insight or vision will emerge. Therefore, it is not too much to say that this insight or value or vision which will emerge from the question-response interaction represents a potential value, a "given" waiting in all situations of our life to be actualized from that interaction. Perhaps this potential which is waiting to be responded to by us is, in one sense, a form of grace or "otherness" which can be discovered if one will let it happen. (This may be a minimum but significant definition of the reality of God.)

There seem to be three possible kinds of interactions between questioner and responder, three categories of possibilities. There is the creative possibility of a creative response, the possibility of unconscious omission, and the possibility of unconscious commission.

A creative question and a creative response is what I want to explore the deepest and I shall return to it later. In itself it implies a tremendously important primary question: what is the condition by which that comes to pass inside me by which I become the kind of person who can creatively ask and creatively respond when asked?

The uncreative omission is the failure to ask the right question when appropriate, or the failure to respond when the right question is posed to us. A very simple example of uncreative omission would be what would happen if a doctor at the scene of an accident did not ask the question "What happened?" If he did not ask *that* question, he could do nothing. Or what happens in human relationship because we fail to ask the question, "What did I do?" And, failing to ask the significant question, we get no insight.

Unconscious or uncreative commission covers the category of situations where one asks either inappropriate questions, or asks them at inappropriate times, or fails to respond, or responds inappropriately when asked the question with all the subsequent consequences. Examples of uncreative commission, in everyday terms, are situations where one intrudes with the wrong questions at the wrong moment, when one interrupts a flow from another person or an interaction between oneself and another person. In human relationships an uncreative commission would be when one is caught in a morbid, lingering self-pitying, "Why did this happen to me?" Or when one intrudes and asks in an inappropriate way, "Why did this happen to you?" or "Why didn't it happen to you?", when it may be none of one's business to ask that of another person. These three categories are just suggestions of ways which could be enlarged on, of possible ways in which "we miss the boat." The categories are not definitive.

Referring to the title *The Eternal Question*, I have spoken on the word "*question*" and have given a few suggestions as to what the idea of questioning really assumes. Let us look now at the word "*eternal.*" What makes or characterizes a question as an *eternal* question? The easiest and most understandable use of the word eternal would be the idea of either a recurring question or a persistent question. An eternal question would be the question that keeps coming back, either in one's own lifetime or throughout history, that recurs or that persists because of its intrinsic value. When I chose this title, what I had in mind was "eternal" as a recurring central question for man or for mankind, repeating itself over and over again throughout history or in a single life. But as I went on, a change came about and I found that what I really meant was a quality of eternity, of the timeless beyond time, which can intersect with time and can change it. The fact that the question is of a timeless quality is what makes it recur and persist. An infusion of the world of time and of history, of our own finiteness, our own ego, with a sense of timelessness, of value beyond our own immediacy — this is the eternal. It is the power of the objective suprapersonal world within and without our psyches, the infusion of the sense of a "Thou" into our limited world, the world of the small "I." From this definition any question is eternal if it is asked by man to that which is more than himself, or is asked by the more-than-himself to himself or to another. It is eternal if the Presence is there.

The eternal question then is a question which has a two-directional possibility. It can be *from* man to the object of devotion (whatever name he gives to it psychologically or religiously) or it can be a question to man from the Thou. The question obviously can take many forms and it may recur, but it does not have to recur or persist in the same form. One could say that an eternal question is any question by man or between men if the central religious archetype of meaning, what Dr. Jung calls the "Self" stands behind or in the question. The eternal question is therefore always concerned with the becoming of something new in one's life or in history. It concerns itself with the ongoingness of value. It is, therefore, purposive and teleological. It is never only causal and reductive but it is forward; it is constructive; it leads to insight rather than statically only to answers. The eternal question is any question either by the conscious ego side to the depths, to the objective psyche within, to the inner timeless world, to the Lord of life, to the great Thou, whatever name you wish to give it, or it is a question asked by that Reality to us. In the words of Eliade, it is the uniting of historical and cosmic time, or for Teilhard de Chardin it is that from which man evolves from a purely biological to a spiritual plane. And this eternal question is possible for man because of the power of reflection or the power of reflective thinking.

Dr. Jung has written:

> "Reflection should be understood, not simply as an afterthought but rather as an attitude. It is a privilege born of human freedom in contradistinction to the composition of natural law. As the word itself testifies, reflection is a spiritual act that runs counter to the natural process, an act whereby one stops, calls something to mind, forms a picture and takes a relation to and comes to terms with what we have seen. It should, therefore, be understood as an act of becoming conscious."

What attitude is required to be a participator in the process of the eternal questioning? Soren Kierkegaard said that "we are so busy cross-examining life, we never stop to let life cross-examine us." And he makes a beautiful statement of the negative:

> "Man often gives himself importance by asking the question which *he* calls the really vital question and he becomes self-important with the thought that he concerns himself exclusively with the vital question, and in so doing, he misses ever hearing the really central question."

That is a very stunning statement. We concern ourselves with the thought that we are concerning ourselves with the vital question and, therefore, we are really missing the opportunity of hearing! We long for seeming certainties and securities of answers which make us miss the real moment where the eternal may be putting to us a significant question.

In the book, *And A Time To Die* by Mark Pelgrin, Sheila Moon has written, "He never begged the Why and Wherefore, the causal and the purposive." There is no area more important than the area of facing our own death or the death of someone else, no area where it is more important to be involved in this process of the eternal question. To be open to this question is by far the greatest assurance that we can round out our life with full dignity.

Many of us were deeply impressed with Ruth Raymond who, at 85 was keeping continually and with great vigilance at this process of confrontation. The booklet *We Drew a Circle*, edited by Luella A. Sibbald, contains many of her insights and struggles with these ever-present questions. She wrote "Our responsibility is to keep at developing through our imagination and our actions creatively and cooperatively by forming, always forming, new images and symbols."

What then is required on the positive side? To be open to people, to one's own inner stillness, to each situation, that one may both *ask* and *receive.*

A dynamic statement from Thomas Mann's novel, *Young Joseph* reads "Thus it must be because one served a God whose nature was not repose and abiding comfort but a God of designs for the future, in whose will, inscrutable, great far-reaching things were in process of becoming and thus was a God of unrest, a God of cares who must be thought for, for whom one must at all times keep oneself free, mobile and in readiness." To keep oneself free, mobile and in readiness is the concrete task of the continual work at those wretched egocentric defenses in us which have to be sacrificed so that fluidity, flexibility and readiness become a characteristic essence of our being rather than a static, defensive system in which most of us operate.

Where do we find the Eternal Question? It may turn up anywhere in life, in any life situation, at any moment of our existence. But it is interesting to ask where we find it in literature and myth. In the great Greek mysteries or in American Indian initiation rites a question is nearly always posed to the initiate before he starts the journey. In the Greek mystery of the Kabeiroi the journier is asked, "What is the worst crime you have ever committed?" In a Winnebago Indian myth one of the instructions to the initiate includes what to say at the end of the rites, when a significant question will be asked. In Wagner's *Parsifal* the hero's whole journey to transformation and redemption is started by the fact that when Parsifal first blunders into the Grail Castle where the wounded Amfortas rules, he fails to ask any question or to answer the question put to him by Gurnemanz. In these mystery rites and many myths, as well as throughout the whole Old and New Testaments, the question is an important, special part of the journey.

I would like now to move to *seven* instances from the field of Biblical dialogue. In each of the instances, we may watch for *who* asks the question, *to whom* it is asked, and *who* does the responding. There is a wealth of instances that could be chosen but these seem especially evocative, real and existential.

Each one of them is a facet of the decisive question of which Dr. Jung speaks when he says:

> "The decisive question for Man is: Is he related to Something Infinite or not? Only if we know that the thing which truly matters is the Infinite can we avoid fixing our own interest upon futility and upon all kinds of goals which are not of real importance."

The *first* instance is from Genesis, Chapter 2, Verse 9 and 10. It is the question, "Where art Thou?" Yahweh asks it of Adam after Eve had eaten of the fruit of the Tree of the Knowledge of Good and Evil and given to Adam from this tree. "The eyes of both were open and they knew they were naked." The Lord God was walking in the cool of the evening and Adam and Eve hid in the garden, but the Lord God called and said, "Where are you?" and Adam answered, "I heard the sound of you in the garden and I was afraid because I was naked and I hid myself."

Here is a primordial myth, a myth about the beginning of things, whether mythologically, evolutionarily speaking or in an individual human life. This is the first step into new consciousness. Man has the first knowledge, the first step toward the ego and, for the moment, he and Yahweh are estranged. Yahweh can't find Man because Man has hidden. Adam cannot face Yahweh because he has obeyed the serpent which may be the other side of God. It is as if Adam is saying, "I am with your other side."

This is an eternal question because of its direct confrontation of Yahweh to Adam, "Where art thou?" At the very individual, personal level, we fear whenever we move into new conscious steps, tiny new steps, or whenever we move out of the blissful state of unconsciousness. All moments of transition are, in one sense, moments of fear, moments of awkwardness and we want to flee, and we are then asked, "Where art thou?" and the question forces us to see our own new stance. Every step toward more inclusiveness means fear and a re-examination of what that step has actually meant to us; we have to resist the temptation to hide when we feel awkward and jittery. We would like to hide from the demands, the challenges, which people and situations put to us when perhaps we have taken the new step which Adam had taken.

The next incident, the *second*, is from Genesis, 4: 8-10, when Cain asks: "Am I my brother's keeper?"

The story is familiar. Abel's sacrifice was accepted by Yahweh and Cain's was not. So Cain murdered Abel and then compounded this evil by being totally irresponsible when Yahweh said, "Where is Abel?" He answered and said, "I do not know. Am I my brother's keeper?"

This question is, of course, particularly significant today, in the light of our relationship to the total social scene. We would prefer so much to remain innocent. We would wish so much that we did not have to say "Yes, I am my brother's keeper." I would like to give you a superb quote from Arthur Miller's play, *After The Fall.* He writes this:

> "*After The Fall* is a dramatic statement of a hidden process which underlies the destructiveness hanging over this age. It throws light upon the inability of man to live with the mixture of good and evil in his own nature."

One of the points of the play is that there cannot truly be a divestment of guilt but there can be and, if life is to be lived, there *must* be a recognition of the individual's part in the evil he sees and abhors. Later, Miller writes, in speaking about the Eichmann trial in Jerusalem:

> "The significant truth about Eichmann is not that he was a monster but that in order to exercise his monstrousness, to be in a position to murder, he had to have the moral permission of others. We were all less than total in our active opposition to barbarity. It is always and forever the same

struggle. To perceive our own complicity with evil is a horror not to be borne; much more reassuring to see the world in terms of totally innocent victims and totally evil instigators of the monstrous violence we see all about us. At all costs, never disturb our innocence.

"What is the most innocent place in any country? Is it not the insane asylum? These people drift through life, innocent, unable to see into themselves at all."

Arthur Miller has, to my mind, put here the tremendous desire and temptation to remain innocent rather than to dare to answer "Yes" to the question and to be willing to move, as Cain was not. There is Cain in every one of us — not only about the outer world but in each one of us about ourselves. To be able to face that Cain, to be able to avoid the temptation of running away, and to be able to move into the real world of time and of historical demand takes genuine responsibility.

The *third* instance is the question from the Eighth Psalm, Verse 3 and 4: "What is Man that Thou art mindful of him and the Son of Man that Thou dost care for him?"

The Psalmist, the man, is asking a question of Yahweh, and out of what does the question come? Why does he ask this question? It comes, perhaps, out of Man's observation at that time, as well as at this time, of his own terrible stupidity, of the fact that Man lets this world fall into such shambles and such destructiveness. Then one looks about and says, "But what is Man that Thou art mindful of him, and the Son of Man that Thou dost care for him?" In spite of what Man does, Man still potentially is something or can be something which is loved, which is sought for by Yahweh and which is, perhaps, needed by Yahweh, because Yahweh or the Eternal longs for a home in Man or else He knows He cannot be known. At a practical level, perhaps whenever we become depressed, whether about ourselves or about our world, whenever we become very bogged down, it may be very good to remember that we are cared for, to remember that if the cosmos is mindful of us, it might not hurt us to be mindful of the cosmos! To get out of our petty, small irrelevant stewing around, which we all go through some of the time, and to be able to ask this question as the Psalmist did, "What is Man—or what am I that Thou art mindful of me?" Here is a reminder that I, Man, am living my life in a framework which has a point of reference and which I must continually remember.

The next instance, the *fourth* one, is from the Book of Job, Chapter 1, Verse 6-8 and is the question "Have you considered my servant, Job?"

Satan, as one of the sons of God, has come to the Lord. The Lord says, "Where have you come from?" and Satan says, "From going to and fro upon the earth and from walking up and down." And the Lord says to Satan, "Have you considered my servant, Job, that there is nothing like him on the earth, a blameless and upright man who fears God and turns away from evil?" or — putting it in other words — "Have you considered this man, Job, who will resist you, Satan, who will not give in to you, and will not give in to the regressive pull that you are but will be able to move forward?" And Satan, of course, goes on to say to the Lord, "Thou hast blessed him" and goes on, "But put forth Thy hand now and touch all that he has and he will curse Thee to Thy face."

Yahweh, here is asking Satan to tempt Job to see if Job will hold up. Will Job remain loyal no matter how difficult the journey? Yahweh is putting a very great question to Satan as if he needed to ask,"Is there a man who can stand the power of the regressive, whether that regressive pull is within man or within Yahweh himself?" "Is there a man, Job, who will resist the temptation to deny? Is there a man who can face darkness in all its forms and stay centered?" This question to Satan is like a dialogue within Yahweh concerning Yahweh's own need that there be a man who can be this conscious. Yahweh is wondering, perhaps, about Man. In the words of MacLeish in his play *J. B.*, this is about man that "scratcheth at the cracked creation." And, of course, the answer in the Book of Job is "Yes." Job does stay loyal no matter what happens and, therefore, a tremendous step of conciousness is achieved. Thus the eternal question here is Yahweh's reflection on whether Man will stay related or whether he will default. At an individual, personal level, what would happen if we put ourselves in Job's place, and if we dared to have Yahweh say to Satan, "Hast thou considered my servant?" and then put one's own individual name there. Have we, have I, have each of us become upright even in the words of the text to withstand regression when dark things assail us, dark things within ourselves, dark things without ourselves — or do we at such moments deny?

I move now to the *fifth* instance to a question from the Gospel of Mark, Chapter 8, Verse 29, where Jesus says to his disciples: "Who say ye that I am?"

Here, Jesus, at the midpoint of his vocation asks his disciples what they think of him and after their answer, he goes on to say who he really feels he is.

This may at first seem only a human question and not an eternal question because it is not obviously between Jesus and God. However, I believe that it is an eternal question because it comes out of an almost continual dialogue which Jesus had with the Father as to who he was as Son. Having rejected his people's images in the wilderness, and being here in process of being rejected himself, he must always ask the question, "Who am I?"

It is the searching of a man to know the exact relation of himself to the divinity he has chosen to serve in the baptism. It is eternal because it is the question which issues from the demands of the Self for Jesus to find his own identity, as each of us must find our identity versus playing a role. It is the attempt to find the boundaries of his own existence through which the eternal resources can flow.

At the individual level, this question raises two issues for us. We have also to let ourselves be asked who we are.

Inside, who are we in our most simple, ultimate, naked reality? How do we find out who we are behind all the roles which people ascribe to us or which we assume as our everyday defenses? Are we only the mother or the father, the teacher, the artist, the psychologist? Is this our essential suchness or must we go on searching? Who say ye that I am in order to find out who am I really? And, secondly, here in this instance, because we are westerners in the western tradition, perhaps we also have to ask the question: Who do we say that *he* is? Who do we say that Jesus is? Middleton Murray, the English writer, says, "Jesus is deep in our bones and our job is to get him out of our bones and into our heads, and then to accept what he has to say or reject it." We are all in the Judeo-Christian tradition, and so we each do have quite individually to answer this question. Who we say that he is may have more to do with who we say we are than could be said of any other central religious figure in our tradition.

The *sixth* question, from Mark 15:34, "My God, my God, why has Thou forsaken me?"

This is a great and a puzzling question that has occupied scholars for 2,000 years, and it may be the most difficult of all the questions.

In 1955 I gave the lecture included in this present book entitled *Analytical Psychology and the Synoptic Gospels* and I made a statement there which aroused more reaction than any other statement in the paper. (I did not then understand the full implication of what I had said.) I said: "This statement, this question, 'My God, my God, why has Thou forsaken me?' may be the utterance of a man in utter agony, a man who knows at this moment that God can do nothing because Man has channeled His, God's power into consciousness and therefore reduced God's omnipotence."

To re-state it: Here is a man, like but beyond Job, who has taken the responsibility for meeting the dark power of himself and of the world, and meeting them with love and taking the responsibility to attempt to transform them.

This moment on the cross may be a moment of the fulfillment of his life in a moment when the dark powers seemed to have triumphed, but we know that something did happen afterwards and they did not triumph. Here, perhaps, God is not helping man but man, this man Jesus, is helping God. The two sides of God have been brought together at this moment into a focused unity of numinous proportion and his cry is that of aloneness, because the Thou whom he has served is himself being transformed by the terrific stature of the "I" of this man. This, perhaps, is the apex and zenith of consciousness.

It is very hard to see or to understand what this could mean individually because it is so far beyond us. But I would wonder if we could ask and try to separate this significant question from moments when we find ourselves calling with self-pity and morbidity, "Why aren't we getting help? Why isn't someone doing something for me?" and the totally different kind of question, of "My God, my God"? Perhaps we approach this kind of question at the moment we come close to the dignity of real suffering. Each of us has a cross within us and each of us, in the words of Paul Tillich, must have the courage to be, which is, perhaps, the courage to be present as an "I" while the "Thou" is also being increased and changed, at the great moment of confrontation.

The last instance is from Luke 1:34 and 35, and the question is, "How can this be, seeing that I know not a man?", the question of Mary to the angel in the Annunciation.

Here is a question that is not about or from Jesus but is, of course, a question inherent in one of the great aspects of the Christian myth as it later grew up around the person of Jesus. This symbolic scene is where the angel, the messenger from God, comes and announces to Mary, as the deep, new, fresh, feminine parts of ourself, that there will be a new child, a new birth, born not from nature, but from supranature, from the work of the Holy Spirit.

I end with this instance because it takes us full circle

back to the first question, "Where art thou?". Adam hid when he lost his innocence, and Mary, another kind of innocence, is afraid but she doesn't hide. Here, if we take this quite inwardly, is some element that is told that she will be the birthplace for some new creation, that there will be an impregnation, and she responds with incredulity but willingness. Here is the breath of freshness, of joy and almost of divine laughter. This is clearly an eternal question because Mary, or the Mary in us, is confronted by the angel, by the messenger, the masculine principle who can come in all sorts of forms and, even though it is hard to believe it, she does not refute it.

This is a question to which we need to be very open and accepting, in order to get behind our fears. We are scared it could happen to us. You know it just might happen — the possibility, for instance, that we could change! It is just possible that something might intervene in the petty, small, defensive, irrelevant life that most of us live, and yet we are thirsting to get out of. It is just possible that something could happen if we would be open. This is a magnificent moment.

Of course, nature does not ask this kind of question. This is the question that is asked by the Mary and the moment when she is confronted by that which is more than nature and when there is the possibility of a great transformation.

At the personal level, as of all of these questions, each person would do well to watch himself and find in some form or another how often, perhaps, he asks the question, "How can this be?"

For our conclusion let us look for a moment at the subtitle of this lecture. The title is *The Eternal Question – What Is It And Who Asks It?* The Eternal Question is the continual emergence of possibility, so needed, when on all sides, we are depressed by the non-caring of Man, by the wreckage that Man is creating in nature and the resources of nature, and the stifling in human relationships. The possibility of the Eternal Question is a possibility of co-creation, the possibility of being a *partaker* in and not a *spectator of*, so that we would go into meaningfulness and depth and not into defeat and meaninglessness.

Who asks it? No *one* asks it. It *is* asked and *we* choose to be in it or not. We choose to be in it, in Thomas Mann's words, "by being free, mobile and in readiness". It is the ongoingness; it is the question which the ongoingness of meaning is continually posing to us.

It is a method that goes back to Socrates, and we speak of it as, in part, a form of the Socratic method. I owe a tremendous debt of gratitude for the development of this method to the scholar with whom I first worked, Henry Burton Sharman. We in the Guild for Psychological Studies have attempted to continue in a similar way. I would like to quote, in reference to a statement which somebody wrote to me after attending a seminar. This person wrote:

"You leaders arouse the one question in the unconscious that we don't want to face, namely the question of God, and you leave everyone to make his or her decision." I would like to think that we often do arouse that question. Apart from method, all of the seminars, whether they are on myth, art, biblical literature, symbol, meditation, are concerned with this matter of the eternal question, are trying to help each individual to find his or her own personal expression of the eternal *in* life and not outside of life.

Finally, we might see this whole process of the Eternal Question as a moving into three points and then into a fourth, which is the matter of wholeness. There is, first of all, the I — the ego — in each of us. There is, secondly, the question posed by me to the Eternal, or posed to me from any source which could be considered eternal. There is the third point, the new point of awareness or insight, forming a triangle between the I, the Eternal and the insightful answer. To see that the living of this insight in substance is the incarnation of the value in the individual forms the fourth point. We need not be waiting for some final apocalypse to be asked the meaning of our lives but, if we really acted on the four steps, we would live every day with this question, "How is it with me in Thine eyes?"

THE ETHICS OF PERSONAL FREEDOM

> "I dreamed that I saw a young child playing with a beautiful apple. The apple was very red and very round and very beautiful. The child was tossing it in the air and enjoying it. I knew in the dream that she should be eating it but she didn't want to eat it."

This dream of a woman patient of mine could be the dream of any of us. Each of us has such a child and such an apple. Each of us is torn by this conflict of whether to let the child play with and enjoy the apple or whether to force the eating. To the dreamer the apple symbolized the fruit of the tree of the knowledge of good and evil. Each of us has this tree in our garden; everything depends on how we use its fruit. Whether we eat and assimilate it, or whether we dally with it, is our choice. Whether, as we stand in the place of our existence, we remain partial people and play with life as a beautiful potential, or whether we get down to business and begin to chew on life and see what happens to us through that process is up to us. This is the meaning of personal freedom.

Where is the circle of our existence? What does our life consist of? What are the general realities of our life? A concrete existence first of all includes the historical time in which we were born. We arrive in a particular moment of history. We are born within a particular nation. We are born of a particular group and we have a certain skin color. We each come into a specific family with its unique family background. Within our family we have complex experiences from the time of our beginnings, sometimes very traumatic experiences which determine and color our future attitudes. We are born with different body builds and different body reactions. These realities are determining factors of our existence. In one sense we can do nothing about them. In addition to all these given realities, we have also the long history of our right and wrong choices, our successes and failures. We have our personal vision, our individual assets, and all of our imperfections and difficulties. These "givens", and the subsequent unfolding acts of our growing, are the circle of our existence, the garden and its fruit.

Everything depends upon what we do within that circle. We can stay inside and make it a vicious circle, a self-perpetuating negative circle about which we can do absolutely nothing. Then we are caught, we say; we are lost; we have simply no power or choice to change anything. On the other hand, we can recognize that we have the chance of changing that self-perpetuating vicious circle into a self-perpetuating magic circle. The burden of predetermined fate can be changed into a gift of destiny, a sense of meaning. Non-acceptance of the realities of our lives can turn into positive acceptance, and thus many of the hurts inside us can be healed.

This personal freedom to choose what we are going to do with the facts of our lives — often very bitter facts, sometimes very wonderful facts, usually some of both — is not something we have but rather is something we are. That is to say, I do not believe we *have* freedom; I think we *are* freedom. We are intrinsically free. Perhaps the margin of freedom is very small, but it is an absolutely crucial margin. We are the struggle for God's freedom. Jacob Boehme, the great mystic, has spoken of God as the original ground of freedom. Whether His wrath or His love is manifested depends on what we do with this. God, for him, is the "Nothing" that wants to become "Something." If we fail to actualize this the Wrath is experienced. If we do actualize this we experience His love.

In the dream of the child and the apple the struggle was between playing with the apple or consuming it, between infantile pleasure and mature assimilation. To take our apples and deal with them creatively is not an easy task, as is clear in the myth of the garden of Eden, the fundamental myth of our Judaic-Christian tradition. And it is the myth not only of our generic cultural-evolutionary development, it is the myth of each individual's development from childhood into adulthood.

What may this myth mean, still speaking in rather large

terms? It means, I believe, that we are all born with a primal wholeness (what Dr. Fritz Kunkel would have called the "primitive we"; what Dr. C. G. Jung called the central "Self"). However, in our personal development, before this wholeness can be made conscious we have to discover our own particular ego, and paradoxically we become split off from our own primal totality through the very process of discovering that ego. Thus man's ego consciousness is a terrible and wonderful acquisition. Certainly the modern world shows us, as perhaps no other time in history has shown, the use of that ego both in the wonder of unbelievable explorations and in the terror of incredible destruction.

How do we play with our gift of ego consciousness? There are so very many ways. We can let our "I" act as if it were separate from its source, and thus fall into Luciferian arrogance. We can try to make the universe conform to the way we would like the universe to be. We can delude ourselves into believing we live in a self-created world. We can let this arrogant "I" manipulate and exploit, can permit it to push people and events outside the limitations of personal reality. We can try to fly with the spirit and forget the substance. We can try to escape with a vision and forget the actuality. We can work at developing ourselves, which in itself is creative to do, but we can do it forgetting where this power for growth comes from in the first place. To misuse the ego, to delude ourselves, to flee limitation — this is what I mean by the lack of personal freedom.

One of the most penetrating statements I know about the problem of freedom is by W. H. Auden in *The Double Man.* Auden writes: "It is possible that the gates of hell are always standing wide open. The lost are perfectly free to leave whenever they like, but to do so would be admitting that the gates were open; that is, that there was another life outside. They know why they do not and this knowledge is a flame of hell." We do not want to face the fact that the gates of hell are always open because if we faced that fact we might have to face also the terrible ethical responsibility of freedom. We would have to accept what Soren Kierkegaard called "the alarming possibility of being able". We would have to take the challenge that Jesus of Nazareth gave to the man sick of the palsy when he said, "Thy sins are forgiven; arise, take up thy bed and walk." All these statements imply the existence of freedom. They imply the need for acknowledging that there is "hell", that there is a pull against possibility, that there is a desire to stay in the bed and not walk. They also imply that it is within man's power of choice to do something to alter his palsied state, or to find the open gate.

I would like to draw on my experience as a psychotherapist and describe a few of the obvious ways in which we avoid facing this fact of personal freedom. Naturally we each have our own particular ways of avoidance and therefore it is not possible to cover all the infinite variations. Let me discuss some familiar ones, not necessarily in the order of their importance.

We avoid facing personal freedom by confining ourselves to philosophical and theological arguments about freedom and determinism. There is a place for philosophy and for theology, but no amount of abstract speculation is as important to individual self-awareness as is facing the determined and the free in one's own life.

Another way that we avoid facing freedom is to stay so frantically busy that we never have time to think about being free and therefore we never have any choices to make because we never sit down long enough to make any. We have no control over life, we say. All the outer circumstances control life because we are caught in the rat race, we say, and therefore we stay very anxious. Anxiety itself is an evasion of the possibility that we could be free of anxiety.

A great number of avoidances of freedom could be subsumed under one-sidedness. We hold grimly onto our partialness instead of trying to find some balance between the conflicting tendencies within us. We stay cut-off and unknowing. We resist psychology, or religious psychology, or anything which might help us to come to more inclusiveness. We protect our inferiority feelings with remarkable zeal. (This is subtle and often takes a long time to detect.) We continually insist, "I have no value within me; I don't have any beautiful apple; I don't have any worth; I'm no good," and so go round and round in a vicious circle of feeling forlorn, put-upon, rejected, thus denying freedom and letting life determine us.

You, I am sure, can add more ways in which we prefer to stay in our neurotic defenses, to let life beat us down, to feel we are helpless, to say that there is no such thing as choice – so I shall not describe others. I suppose a psychotherapist perhaps more than most people has a chance to see how fundamentally ambivalent man is about freedom. Patients often ask, when I speak of resistance to growth, "Why would I come to an analyst if I didn't want to change and grow?" Surely they want to change and grow, but only with part of themselves; another part resists. And resistance in the most primary sense means not only fear of the negative facts but also fear of those creative facts through which one could change, such as the fact that the gates of hell are wide open for departure as soon as a genuinely ethical choice is made.

The chief question is, then, how can one begin to act in order for the choice-making factor in the personality to be affirmed, exercised, used? How can one begin to assume responsibility for life? A few years ago a friend pointed out to me how the word "responsibility", if taken apart, becomes "response-ability", the ability to respond. You could, then, begin to make choices and to be free by beginning to respond and react differently from the way you always have. To start asking yourself a series of questions, and to listen for individual answers, is a beginning. Listen way down inside yourself for your own answer, and live with the answer until you hear new questions out of the answer. Suppose each of you started with questions such as the following: How do I see my world? Do I perceive truly? Is there anything that I have perceived in my real world today? Not glanced at, but absorbed? Have I responded today to anything? Did I see the mountain with the snow when the sun broke through for a few moments? Did I see the new buds that are aching to be born? Did I enter into the dogginess of the dog, the cattiness of the cat, the freshness of the child, the smile of the friend? Did I know the cat, the dog, the child, the friend were there or did I pass them by? Did I ask of these things what they want me to ask of them? Dr. Jung has used the phrase "the claim of the object". Did I respond to this claim?

Most of us are so isolated in our little prison that we never stop to ask such questions. Getting beyond this tight bind of egocentricity is related to what Martin Buber (who has profoundly influenced my own thinking) calls the "I-Thou" relationship. Buber's "I-Thou" involves not only relating to persons, but also to a more inclusive range of subjects. I can perceive anything, animate or inanimate, either as a "Thou" or as an "It". And in Buber's terms, most of the time I see everything as an "It". This is neurotic perception. Such perception is a result of not letting go of defenses. We do not dare to let ourselves be vulnerable enough to permit an "It" to become a "Thou" and let it speak to us, because if we did the "Thou" might say something that would alter us in the process, and we are afraid to be altered. Yet at the same time we want very much to be changed. When difficulties, darkness, objective or subjective suffering or pain come to us we tend, out of self-protection, to block ourselves from them and to say, No! You mustn't touch me! How much more creative it is to welcome them and say, Yes, you're here for some reason that I don't understand, but I must let you speak to me. Do we dare to do that? Do we take time thus to nourish ourselves and the deeper life within us? Do we make the effort to become the kind of person who can respond wholeheartedly, courageously, freely to life's events?

There is a brief poem, "And No Bell Rings", by Josephine Johnson which reads:

> Some day, when all the little bills are paid,
> And all the letters answered, and the door

Chained and bolted, and the chair
Propped under the handle, and no bell
Rings:
In that day we will rise and walk to the window,
We will rise and kneel by the window,
And observe the mountains where the eagles nest.

I believe that we have to reverse the process described here if we are to discover personal freedom. If we wait for a time when all the bills are paid and all the letters answered and the door chained, I wonder if we will ever get to kneel and to look at the mountain where the eagles nest. Must we not, rather, choose oftentimes to put aside the bills and all they symbolize, the letters and all they symbolize, and take time to kneel and to look out the window, whatever this act symbolizes to us? Modern life is so constituted that the time for kneeling does not come very naturally, and perhaps only if we are strong in our affirmation of freedom will we make the time. I am sure what the poet is urging is that we attend to the fundamental values rather than spend all our energies on the necessities. Of course the bills must be paid and the letters must be answered. These are facts which determine our lives. We do, however, have a margin of choice as to how we apportion our energy.

Another category of questions that could be asked in exploring the ethics of personal freedom has to do with self-acceptance. Can I look at my own shortcomings? Can I look at my own imperfections and liabilities and accept them without guilt? Can I open my arms to them and say, This is the way I was. I wish I hadn't been that way, but this is the way I was. This is the way I am. At the other pole, can I also look at the positive things in me? Can I accept not only the horrors but also the glories? Can I see the assets as well as the liabilities? Can I acknowledge that I am a mass of opposing forces? If I am selfish one minute, I am unselfish the next. If I am sensitive and perceptive today, I may be insensitive and unperceptive tomorrow. Nothing is static and nothing is certain. I am in a state of continual flux. This is how I *am* the struggle. When I face my world and the things in it that happen to me, do I call these happenings accidental, or do I go deeply enough to know my world as purposive? Do I label events involving me as only negative deterministic circumstances, or am I able to see everything that comes to me as having in it a hidden message if only I am creative enough to ask the right question?

Response to the world, acceptance of individual identity – these are the two areas I have covered in discussing questions to ask in order to indicate where and how one can choose freedom. There are innumerable further questions, and each person will discover his own. Asking the questions does not change matters suddenly, but it may be the beginning of a long, slow, painful, and wonderful process by which something could really happen.

A further step is now necessary, for if man is neither a predetermined puppet nor an unrestricted god, where does he turn for the resources both to ask the questions and to listen for answers? I believe these resources are to be found deep inside ourselves. We must then, as Dr. Jung points out, go willingly to the creative resources within. Goethe said, "In the dangerous element immerse." Why is it dangerous to plunge into our creative resources? It is so because we cannot turn inward to find newness without being willing to sacrifice old patterns. This is a necessary but difficult sacrifice, for we are most reluctant to give up the static inflexible images which we have worked so hard to achieve. Jesus addressed himself to this problem often, but most strikingly in those parables where in various ways the true pattern of being is described as new wine, as the stranger coming in the night or the bridegroom at midnight. In other words, we have to be willing to leave the known, the usual, the illumined, and go to the greatest darkness to find the healing elements. As T. S. Eliot has written, "What you do not know is the only thing you know."

These kinds of formulations are difficult for us to understand and encompass, not only because we are inflexible and have built up monstrous ego defenses, but also because they are ideas more or less foreign to our Western religious culture. To find new light in black midnight involves the affirmation of the feminine principle, and especially in Protestantism we know very little about the feminine side. Mary is not a central figure of worship. We have essentially a masculine Judaic-Christian tradition. We are inheritors of Puritanism. We are unfamiliar with the idea of descending into our own substance, there to discover something of God. We have very little in our religious tradition to help us to go inward to find what the Quakers call the "inner light". And how alien it generally is for those of us who have been brought up in Protestantism actually to pray to a feminine aspect of the deity who could help us to get into the roots — into the earth. How alien it feels to turn not to father sky but to mother earth, our own inner mother earth, or own inner substance, in order to restore the wholeness of the individual psyche.

The paradox is that the very thing we have worked so hard to achieve in our cultural evolution — this ego consciousness, this sense of "I" — now must reverse itself and renounce its claim to be independent and go back to its source. It must acknowledge a new master. In the words of Fritz Kunkel, we must become willing to become "co-creators". We must not just be creative off here by ourselves. We must develop all we can of our own individuality. But this is possible only when we come full circle back to the source out of which we originally were born. The Chinese say, "To be battered is to be renewed." We must be willing to have all the things which we have been so concerned to build up with our prideful ego laid low so that a new structure can arise. We must be all we can be, and when we are all that we can be we must in one sense become nothing.

Why is it important what I do with my life? Not only for myself but for God and, I would say, for history. Why is it crucial whether I choose to become a truly conscious person or remain isolated?

The great German poet Rainer Maria Rilke spoke to

this question dramatically when he wrote:

> What will you do, God, if Death takes me?
> I am your jug (if someone breaks me?)
> I am your drink (if curdling cakes me?)
> I am your trim, your trade — it makes me
> think; with me goes your meaning too.
> Your cloak will slip from off your shoulders.
> Your glance, which on my cheek would rest,
> warmly as by a pillow pressed,
> will come, and, after much vain quest,
> sink, as the sun goes down the west,
> into some lap of alien boulders.
>
> What will you do God? I'm distressed.

This is Rilke's way of saying how much God needs man, how much man's choice of what he does with his life determines not only his own life but the fulfillment of God. In Rilke's thought God is the creator; He is the answer to the mystery, but He obviously needs co-creators. And Rilke says, what will God do when man is not here to express His purpose. Shocking and radical, to be sure, but well worth thinking about. It is urgent for the on-goingness of purpose, of meaning, and of value in the world that we do work at achieving personal freedom and make decisions of how we use it. Another way, I suppose, of putting it is to say that it is urgent that we become true pilgrims.

I have had the great privilege of visiting Greece and going to all the places where the Greek mysteries had been enacted and ritualized over a period of approximately one thousand years, from about 500 B.C. to 500 A.D. I was deeply impressed as I felt into what were the rites of initiation that went on in these mysteries. We have nothing in our culture comparable to them, nothing in our religion comparable. Contemporary primitive tribes do have something of initiation rites for different inner developments, but we so-called "civilized" individuals have the almost superhuman problem of developing some way by which we can become initiated into the deeper inwardness that lies beyond the purely conscious side of ourselves.

By our own choices, by our affirmation of freedom and our acts toward wholeness, we may perhaps be able to change the circle of our existence from one in which we feel pursued into one where we feel there is purpose. In T.S. Eliot's play, *Family Reunion*, there is a point at which the hero, Harry, is trying to solve a family problem and is being pursued by the Eumenides, the Greek fates. At the moment of his turning towards his own personal meaning, the Eumenides change their dark visages and Harry says, "I must follow the bright angels."

That is what I am in part trying to discuss. By conscious psychological work on ourselves we change our dark fates to the bright angels, those helpful healing forces which are present in the psyche (and outside as well) wanting to help us if we will let them. This then is true reversal of direction. It is a choice whereby one wins a new freedom. By using this personal freedom then, perhaps paradoxically, freedom is attained for the first time.

Whether in the statement from the Gospel of John "Ye shall know the truth and the truth shall make you free", in the words of Paul, "In loving bondage free", or in the teaching of Jesus stating, "Whosoever shall lose his life shall save it", it is clear that freedom has two sides — personal ego responsibility and submission to a greater purpose. If we develop the potential affirmations of life and consciousness, and submit them to the deeper powers, then we will have the sense of very great purpose and very great freedom. That is, not by stepping *outside* our life, which most of us are desperately trying to do, but stepping *into* our life, we become free.

A centered, rooted person stands ever and eternally in the midst of a flux of changing conditions, inner and outer, assaulted by winds and storms, but ready to function. All decision and choice, at its best, reflects an understanding of, and relationship to, one's own inner processes, realized and unrealized and, at the same time, an awareness of the demands of the outer real situation. An authentic personality has a frame of reference for morality in the concrete, springing from deep sources, yet always referring to the actual world of time and reality. Its source may be called eternal but it only functions in application to the world of humanness, limitation and temporality. For it is in the concrete world that a person lives, has his being, and expresses himself. There is a statement in the Jewish mystical tradition which says that "Man was created for the sake of choice." Choices are forever pressing us, and the centered person has a criterion of value from which to gauge and measure his decisions, which will be the expression of himself and yet will include all those factors and people involved in each decision.

Today we are in a period where there are no clear-cut absolute standards, but rather a time characterized by flux and anxiety. Nevertheless, sound individual bases must be found from which insight, courage and decisiveness issue. In the words of Jesus of Nazareth, the man whose house is "built on rock", suggesting something sound, firm and beyond assault, was never more needed nor more difficult to find. However, during the process of the achievement of such a "fruit" of centeredness or maturity, many problems of an ethical and moral nature present themselves to all seekers, including the analysand and the analyst.

Exactly what are these problems? In the course of analytic treatment, as well as in self-searching, many elements from the unconscious are released and brought to the threshold of consciousness. When these dynamic elements begin to come up, whether through dreams, or through and in life-situations, they demand attention and action. Having been repressed since childhood and covered up by all the ego mechanisms designed to "keep them down" they become autonomous, powerful and influential, though covert. Although many of them may turn out to be positive and valuable for the personality, they usually have the character of seeming inconsistency with the conscious, approved side. As they begin to rise to consciousness, what does one do about them? How integrate them? How bring them into positive relatedness that honors one's other sides but does not just blindly neglect the realities of other people? This same question arises whether one speaks of the Id (sexual impulses) of the Freudians, or the divine, non-animal elements which Jung includes within the unconscious. The problem remains: How does one know what to do about them? What are the risks involved in their recognition? How treat them so that they do not become inner "step-children" but fully a part of an inner democratic process? This presents itself as a problem whether dealing with hostility and aggressiveness, of the qualities of repressed compassion and tenderness. Does one automatically express them, regardless of outcome? Does expression always assure integration? Does one suppress them, judging them as "evil", and relegate them again into the basement?

Is it possible that there is a third way — an "ethical" and creative though positively dangerous way in which the growing discrimination of how to deal with them in itself is therapeutic, apart from what one does with the specific content being dealt with? Through this a growing moral sensitivity comes. The problem is a deep and difficult one. Examples abound. The individual discovers that he hates his mother with whom he is living. Does he pretend to her that he doesn't? Does he tell her that he does? Does he try to talk it over with her? Does he get violent with her? Does he try to use some art-form, as painting or clay, to release and objectify his emotions? And so on and so on. The answer is not immediately self-evident, because the ordinary category of our ethics based on repression is not satisfying. An analyst does not have the answer, and it is not in books. Rather, delicately, in a highly individual and unique fashion, analyst and analysand together must attempt to find the "right" answer. And what is meant by "right" here? That action may be seen as best which is based on the greatest degree of insight for the person's growing self-fulfillment, yet holding in balance the consideration of the existence of other persons.

A married woman falls in love with a married man. It is real to her, somewhat real to him. Does she repress it, following all the taboos surrounding the area of sexuality in our culture? Does she admit it to herself and her analyst and try to work out some symbolic expression of it? Does she share it with her husband? Does she live it out in an overt way with the interested man? Does she divorce her husband? How does she pay respect to all the values that she is trying to maintain in herself, including a new value relative to which there must be some choice? How does she answer the question as to why the event happened anyway? What does it mean in both these cases to try to avoid the negative dangers of either extreme — irresponsible "licentious" action with blindness to all consequences, or action dominated by rigid defense systems which have assumed an ethical character but which are quite divorced from psychological reality?

Another kind of example may help. Take the case where there comes the discovery that all of one's social and political liberal opinions are colored by neurotic tendencies, subliminations of rebellion against the parental patterns. As these patterns begin to assume some conscious character, what happens to the opinions? Seeing their neurotic basis, does this invalidate them? Does one withdraw from all social actions? Does one throw one's self into the opposite camp? Does one take on ever more intense activity? Again, there are no written answers. Painfully one must work through the problem, with its full implications that, especially here, have great social import.

We are so pulled apart that the "right" becomes identified exclusively with defense and approval patterns, or we are pulled by the desire to go completely in the "wrong" direction, having as yet no real criterion as to which is which where we literally may know nothing of the meaning of values except as intellectually held ideas, where we are "lost in the dark". Such problems exist, according to Jung, because we are the victims of an enormous split between the conscious and unconscious, the rational and irrational sides of our nature. In this split, what concerns us is that our ethics have become identified with this rational and often conventional side. Thus what we are trying to live are ideas-about, or intuitions-about, things, leaving the power of the real motive for action unexpressed and lying unused in the unconscious. In religious language, we have left out vast areas of ourselves in our reckoning as to who and what we are. We have thus unconsciously identified God with the known rigid ideals, leaving the irrational side to the "devil" within. Being thus dualistic, we have lost any deeply-rooted sense of value, security and moral functioning. Having left out of account the actual facts of the psyche, thus limiting our perception, our choices are inadequate.

To begin to change ethical perception from standardized, crystallized systems and in some way to include more of the totality, is a huge shift, a fundamental change in the field of ethics, but one which cannot be overlooked. It means (and it sounds so simple, like all great things) that decisions about right and wrong must be made individually in the light of one's knowledge of one's self and one's environment and not exclusively on that of established laws. This does not rule out, however, the validity and contribution of the inherited body of wisdom of the centuries. It says that we must take the risk and be individuals finding our own meaning and interpretation. This is difficult. It challenges the approach that is deep in our bones, that of depending on outer authority. It also assumes a possibility of self-respect and a sense of dignity, very hard to find in the psyche of those of us ridden by self-hatred and mutilation. Is there any element in us which can be trusted in the midst of all the conflicting tendencies of our nature?

At this point Dr. Jung has made a significant contribution. He has indicated that in each person there is to be discovered a potential called the Self, which is a deeper and more inclusive center of totality than the personality. This Self, a postulate that has grown out of empirical observation, has about it an ethical character, and when touched and made accessible to the person forms the basis of choices more sound than those based only on the ego. Gerhard Adler, in his book *Studies in Analytical Psychology*, says that "our conscience, our inner moral and ethical laws, our inner voice, or whatever else one may like to call these formative factors are due to *a priori* conditions of the human psyche — they are manifestations of the Self." To find the Self, then, is really to discover the answer to our dilemna about values. But, again, what does all this mean during the process of analysis, when certainly the real Self has not yet been touched, and one is in the midst of these uprising conflicting elements? It assures us that there *is* something to be found, and that it is constructive. It means, however, that we will find ourselves at times with no clarity as to what is "right"; it assumes that often what will seem to be "wrong" may not be so when looked at with a new perspective; it begins to put ethics where they belong, within the framework of psychological and religious reality.

What is the analysand up against during this process? And what is the attitude of the analyst? What the analysand brings to the analytic situation, in bringing himself, is in part his established patterns and his repressions. These may vary from a case where there is complete domination by a "Christian" ideal of inhibition and repression, preventing any insight and action, to the extreme where any sense of control is overcome by the power of the inner drives. His parental patterns may still be the dominant ones — or he may be rebellious against them. He may be a passive or an aggressive person. He may be naturally sensitive, or he may be somewhat callous and insensitive. But during the process he stands revealed to himself with new facets of his personality which will sometimes bring pain and sometimes joy. His insight into himself and others will grow. The slow rebirth of his personality begins with the shatterings and tumblings of the old standards, and this is a devastating time of being "between two worlds". It is in this difficult time, often of long duration and before any real sense of value-discrimination is there, that certain attitudes are needed and where the analyst helps. In this betwixt and between period of purposiveness and yet direction-lessness the analysand needs courage. It is a period where blunders and mistakes will be made. The growing new point of orientation may force one to hurt others, or to endure and to inflict conflict which one has always avoided. One may for one's own self-development have to do certain illegitimate, unorthodox things.

The non-canonical statement attributed to Jesus, when his disciples were plucking fruit on the Sabbath is, "Blessed art thou if thou know what thou doest." Everything depends on the degree of consciousness with which one performs an act – even one that is against the established custom. In so acting, one has to be willing to make mistakes and to take the consequences. In the same way, one has to do what is indicated in the analysis without guilt, and humbly. Of course guilt is there, it is inevitable – but one must begin to face it and to try to see that the thing being done must be done for the sake of life itself. If the seemingly insensitive, hurtful act, for the moment producing misunderstanding, is seen as a process and not as an end product, different results accrue. It is infinitely more desirable to get into some kind of action rather than to remain neurotic and inactive. The first little step of action to break patterns has danger inherent in it, but how much less dangerous than to do nothing!

During this trying time, the analyst should be accepting – not merely in words but in reality – participating, objective, trying to help the person to become responsible, holding perhaps a tentative idea but never imposing it. But above all, he must help the awareness-process for the patient, especially at times of decision-situations. He has to let the patient make mistakes; he cannot save him from that. Deeper even, he cannot save him from suffering. He can stand with him, supportive yet independent. Only so can he give aid so that a new personality may be born who learns what to do, when to do it, and what not to do, who learns what to sustain and what to give way to, who knows when to speak and when to keep silent, when to consider others and when to consider himself. In this way a new person may evolve, a choosing, positively ethically-oriented one whose inner and outer life cohere, and in whom there is integrity.

With this awareness man can "incarnate" God through himself, can fulfill meaning in his body, in his reality, on his own ground. The powers entrusted to him must be returned to the source from whence they came. He never owned them in the first place, although he lives a good many years on the assumption that he does. He is always essentially a servant of life, but he has forgotten that he is here in order to serve. If he remembers these things of freedom, he may become the kind of person of whom Josephine Johnson has written, at the end of her poem, "Let Go. Return.":

> Behold, he has done one thing well,
> And he knows whereof he speaks, and he means
>   what he has said,
> And we may trust him.
> This is sufficient for a life.

FORGIVENESS AS WOUND AND HEALING

The problem of forgiveness is the problem of wounds. It is the problem of wounds received and wounds given. It is hurts done to us knowingly and unknowingly, and it is the hurts inflicted by us knowingly and unknowingly. It has been said that "we are our scars." Out of the wounds often hidden, forgotten, ignored or repressed, come sins, done to us and done by us in the past and in the present to other people. These sins come out of our neglected wounds. Forgiveness is the knowledge that there is a power — a resource — which can help us to meet, to encounter, to heal these wounds and these sins through love and genuine and deep acceptance, not through repression. Forgiveness in the words of Paul Tillich is the "acceptance of the unacceptable." It is reconciliation in spite of estrangement and alienation. In the words of T.S. Eliot, in *Family Reunion*, forgiveness is the process by which "the crooked may be made straight" and "the knot may be unknotted" and the "crossed may be uncrossed".

The psychological problem is how to evoke these wounds and these sins so often forgotten, done to us and by us, without dwelling on them or getting lost in them morbidly. The religious problem is how to intercept this power or this resource with these wounds and these sins so that they may be transformed and reconciled and brought into love and growth. Forgiveness is not to do away with the problem of evil but to admit its existence and by including it to have an opportunity of transforming it. We defeat the hurt, the sins and the split, only by acceptance and by being accepted. Otherwise we are left with a chasm in ourselves which leads to a sense of emptiness and loss. We have the freedom to be or not to be in this process of forgiveness. We can choose whether to work to transform our lives into some singleness, healing and unification, or we can choose to stay apart from the process, from ourselves and other people, to stay fragmented — to stay autonomous — and full of unsolved problems. I would like to make five points and examine each one deeply, hoping that they will be provocative to you about this problem in which we need involvement. It is one of the crucial problems of our age. As we look around the world today it is not a pleasant world; it often has not been pleasant but it most certainly is not so now. It could be beautiful but it is not. We need to be involved in deep problems of self searching, of searching in regard to our relation to other persons, our relation to groups, and our membership in larger social groups.

The problem of wounds which have been done to us and done by us is where we must start. The deepest level behind our sins is the problem of our hurts. It is the most ignored and the most forgotten area, and perhaps it is the one actually to which such religious psychologists as Dr. Fritz Kunkel and Dr. Carl Jung have made their greatest contribution. Because this wounded material has been repressed and forgotten and ignored forgiveness must start with its uncovering. Behind it, behind the negative there *is* the creative power. This makes the difference between religious and non-religious psychotherapy. The question of what we genuinely know, in the deepest sense of that word, is the purpose of opening up our negative. Is it just to get the negative parts of ourself out into the open, or is it because we *know* that if we face the negative, then in fact there is something at work which wants to be born and which wants to come into life, into fulfillment and into consciousness? This latter I would call a religious attitude. If we do not face these early hurts that have been done to us, they fester; they get covered over.

We have to face the fact that these hurts which originally have been done to us originated with parents, at least in part. Every one of us has been at one time or another a child. Some of us have had very difficult parents and some of us have had extremely well meaning parents. Sometimes the very well-meaning ones have turned out to be destructive and negative ones. They were well-intentioned but they simply did not always know the negative depths of the things which they were doing. Perhaps the parents of today—the new generation—have a great chance and opportunity because they do have more psychological insights than the very well-meaning parents of my generation. If these hurts are not dealt with inside ourselves they then get projected into other situations when we are adult and we then also hurt other people and we react inappropriately to them. Sometimes we imagine that they hurt us, and sometimes in actual fact they do hurt us, but in either case we must be able to face it and to do something about it. The reason we are so hurt so often as adults is because we have not yet faced what Robert Raynolds, in his excellent book *The Choice to Love*, calls "the despised and rejected child who dwells in the heart of each of us all our life long." We must face and deal with this child, as adults, and it is not easy to face this child inside us because it means giving up so many of our egocentric self-images. We see ourselves as people who have supposedly achieved maturity, and many of us hope we are on the route to responsibility. We have taken our place in the adult world—and yet we know all sorts of symptoms and reactions which are quite disproportionate to the situation—and these may come because in our unconscious we are carrying this despised and rejected child and we have never had the courage to look at this child, let alone really to deal with it.

Secondly, if we leave these hurts and these wounds unheeded they then fester, become angry, and produce in us hostility and meanness and negativity. Before we know it we are committing sins and hurts to other people. We do it personally a good deal of the time, sometimes without meaning to and sometimes, of course, we do mean it! And our personal lives are compounded into the social body—the social psyche—so the symptoms of violence and hatred are tearing us apart in our country and in our world. The angry breakdown of communication between peoples is certainly the reflection of the breakdown of communication in ourselves, the lack of cohesiveness in ourselves and the lack of a very genuine loving "I-thou" relationship, between friends, husbands and wives, parents and children.

There is a quotation in the book of the newly discovered apocryphal Gospel of Phillip, a statement attributed to Jesus, which says "For so long as the root of wickedness is hidden — it is strong, but when it is recognized it is dissolved." It is so very much easier of course to see the root of wickedness out there in everybody else, in all "those others", individual and groups instead of really facing that the wickedness I participate in comes by the very nature of being human. The title of one of Dr. Jung's most valuable books, in regard to the relation of the personal and social situation, is *The Undiscovered Self.* The very title speaks of the fact that there is a Self—a deep self which we have not discovered in ourselves. The reason we have not discovered it is that we not only have outer iron curtains between us and other countries, but because we have iron curtains inside ourselves, and these iron curtains keep us compartmentalized so that "the right hand knoweth not what the left hand doeth." In another non-canonical book, the *Gospel of Thomas*, it states "Let him who has become rich become king and let him who has power renounce it." We knew at the time of the tremendous tragedy of the John Kennedy assassination that behind Oswald the murderer there was a lonely, cold, alienated child and that he represented this very process I am talking about. The possibility of the depths of the original hurt and wound having festered and become angry enough to lead to that tragic murder. Another striking example of what happens outwardly socially, when we repress the hurt places, was the picture of Washington, D.C. in flames after riots there which came out of Martin Luther King's assassination. A cloud of dark heavy smoke lay across the White House, symbolizing the center of power, surrounded by anger and hostility finally coming out of the black people's frustration when Dr. King's non-violence was no longer there as a buffer between black and white. We know that those people are starved and neglected because we have left our own dark side unappeased and unfed and projected it outside so that these black people reflect our own hidden dark parts which have become angry. They have a right to be angry, just as the blacks do.

We know the nastiness of a man and a woman to one another because they cannot admit that hurt is there. In one sense it is much easier to be angry, much easier to fight, and sometimes it is healthy to do so. But certainly anger needs to be transformed.

And this leads to the third point. These wounds, our forgotten side, become our sins, and forgiveness is based on the knowledge of a power – a resource – that helps us transform the problem – helps us in the words of Tillich to overcome our self disgust. Whatever the name, this resource is present; it is a Presence. It is a "given"; it is an *a priori* numinous "given" in the nature of things, and we can experience it. We know we are experiencing it when we have decreased tension, opened up of our heart, and found a clarity of mind. Some people will call this resource God, some will call it Christ, some will call it Jesus, some will call it Tao, some will call it the Self. There are many people today who need new terms for it, not because the old terms are not good, but because in the current religious revolution people want to get to the realities behind the terms which have lost their meaning. Many people today would speak of the resource in Buber's terms – as "the great Thou." Psychologically one may say "the integrative force", or the force which makes for integration. In the words of Teilhard de Chardin it is the thrust of evolution moving forward toward convergence, and psycho-genesis, and planetization, as opposed to divergence and people being torn apart. One of the great American poets, May Sarton, says in one line of her poetry "there is in each of us a healing mother."

Whatever its name, there is that which is at work in the Universe, that which is at work in the psyche of man – to bring about order and restoration out of chaos – to bring love out of hate – that which makes for integration instead of that which makes for disintegration – with its Presence. Whatever name we give it, it affirms itself if we move with it. It affirms the "yes" over the "no", and it affirms life over death. It comes every moment not in a system but as a potential experience, if we open ourselves to that experience. Certainly one of the reasons so many people today are not in the *process of forgiveness* (which is the way I would put it), is because they feel that some of the old terms do not include the totality of what is inside themselves.

We come to the fourth point. How do we evoke that which is hurt, forgotten, wounded inside us? We must do so, in the interests of integration, wholeness, redemption; for if we do not there is a heavy price to be paid by ourselves and other people. But how now do we do this? I would like to bring the contribution of analytical psychology to this question in its religious depth. The religious and the psychological must be together. The science and art of psychology has some specific approaches to make, to the problem of meditation, introversion, prayer, which can be helpful. Forgiveness always implies looking at these things inside ourselves, in the Presence of that which is greater than myself. What are some of the ways that I can evoke these things? The whole field of therapy and analysis of course is centered in this, (including dream interpretation), but I am not concerned with the professional aspect here. There are things which we as individuals can do if we have courage, if we are committed enough, if we really have some genuine passion (and how few of us have any passion about anything today!). We have never so much needed the passion for living and for convergence and wholeness, not only in our personal lives but in the world. So how may we evoke it?

Let me begin with such a very simple thing as to begin to be honest. This sounds extremely simple, very easy to say and so difficult to do. For instance you can begin such a simple thing as to keep a journal and write down some of your reactions. Not "I went to see my sister today or I called on my friend" unless something happened when you saw your sister or your friend! But rather "This was a feeling I had today – these were the reactions I had" and really write in such a way that you know that no one except you and God, you and the Presence will see it. Otherwise inner people come in as censors, and even then you will have a censor who will come in and say "You shouldn't have felt that today. That's a naughty feeling, a bad feeling." But you did have it. It was an honest-to-goodness feeling – a reaction – perhaps it was a nasty one, but it has to be faced if it is a part of our wholeness. This is not a negative self-centeredness. It is an attempt to suggest some very simple, concrete things which are concerned with the religious journey—the religious journey by which one becomes a more whole and complete person, living with a sense of moving with the "will of God" in the words of Jesus, moving with that which is of deep and everlasting value. So be honest, write out letters but do not send them to people whether they are living or dead, but write them because they express something! Many people have had to write letters to people who were no longer present, because it helped to see or to discharge an inner infection that was festering, producing fears and anxieties, fears about illness, old age, fears about death of someone, fears about the dark, fears about almost anything. But these things have to be brought out, they have to be faced, so writing about them helps. But write seriously. It is necessary to be completely serious.

More difficult, probably, for some to face is to be willing to paint, get a piece of clay, do something in art, not because you are an artist but mainly because it is a way to get at the inner world. Or perhaps you have a picture that you love and you look at it, in addition to what you may make. In either case you have a chance to really see, to perceive in symbolic form inner problems and to look at them. Then one can do something about it. One can work with it somehow.

These simple things are a few ways of taking the soul seriously. Dr. Jung has helped us to see that one of the terrible modern problems is that we no longer take the soul seriously. We do not take inwardness seriously. (Of course, we should not take inwardness to the deprivation or the detriment of the outer world where we also live.) We are constantly making decisions, choosing values, relating every day, but we must take our inwardness seriously for otherwise we are less than total people and our decisions are affected. These, then, are ways to be willing to feel the pain, the hurt, to be open, to be vulnerable, to be willing to overcome, to sacrifice our egocentric self-images, our illusions, and to face what Dr. Jung has called our shadows, and some of the opposites within ourselves. Arthur Miller, the author of the play *After the Fall* said this: "There cannot truly be a divestment of guilt but there can be, and if life is to be lived there must be, a recognition of the individual part in the evil he sees and abhors." These simple suggestions are attempts to get at the potential evil which resides in our heart and which must be looked at and faced and struggled with.

Lastly, if I look at some of these things and begin to know them, then how do I work with them, how do I bring them into forgiveness? How do I intersect or come into contact with this power, this source, this reality, which can help to transform them and to change them? This raises the central questions which must be answered. Who forgives? What do I need to forgive? What do I need to be forgiven for? Whom do I need to forgive? What needs to be forgiven, what needs to be forgiven in me, what and where are the resources of forgiveness and what is the role of creative guilt in forgiveness? There *is* a position held by many with which I profoundly disagree. I do not think that I forgive. I do not think we forgive. I think rather that the task is to bring what I find in myself and in my relationships to that Reality where I can experience forgiveness. That is very different from saying "I forgive." The danger of saying "I forgive" is great, because it can be extremely inflated. The very statement of it has a terrible danger of arrogance in it, a sort of "I, the great giver of forgiveness." I am not the forgiver—*I must participate in that which is making for forgiveness, or at least I must try to.* My task is to bring with repentence that which I have done, that for which I am responsible, and I must also bring that which has been done to me. I must bring both of them into a sense of Presence. In the words of Jesus, I must bring my anger to the altar. And I must find the altar wherever I can find it. It may be at eleven in the morning in a church or at any other time. It may be in my own home. It may be in some very personal symbol. But wherever it is, I must bring my unacceptability and my self-disgust and my guilt to a place where I can feel that it can be accepted, whatever symbol for the transforming power I may use. I must bring it and I must be ready to face that the results of what I have done, or what has been done to me will not be eradicated but altered, and energy released. I will be in one sense "punished" but not judged. I use "punished" in the sense that there *are* actually results from things; but that is very different from saying I will be judged. I will work to bring out these negative things, not to keep them down. I will work to bring them, to transform them into love. I must not work with love on one side and the negative things over on the other. This is the split that most of us have had. I will try with as much wholeness as my two hands can make, to embrace all that I have and know and to present it to the altar—to present it to that which symbolizes acceptance by God.

I would like to share with you a dream of a patient that is a beautiful dream of forgiveness. Not everyone is privileged to have this kind of dream. It's a dream of a woman who had worked a long time in analysis. I will not go into her problems here. I will simply say that she dreamt she went into a garden, and in the garden there was a small old dwarfed man who was very hateful and very hostile towards her, and she felt that he meant to do her harm. At first she started to turn, and then she thought better of herself and she turned and went to him even though he was very evil looking. She went up to him and she put her arms around him and said the Lord's prayer, and he broke into tears. This is a classically beautiful dream of what I am trying to communicate. This woman had the insight of the moment in her dream, to meet what looked to be and what was in fact an evil, aggressive, angry, hostile thing, with love and with a religious presence, and because she did, that which was angry and cruel and hostile burst into tears. This is the same theme which one finds in many legends and fairy tales, namely that that which is negative in the story turns out to have been bewitched. So the frog turns into the beautiful prince. It is not accidental that the fairy tales say that. It is because this is the way it happens, so that behind what looks sometimes like kind of unattractive frogs in our lives, if we can love them—if we can encompass them (it is a big "if"!) with a sense of presence, they may turn out to be the beautiful prince or princess.

But that woman was a religiously committed woman

because she knew to bring the Lord's prayer. When the unconscious knows the Lord's prayer as well as the conscious, then there is really movement. I would like to amend a statement which was on a Church program recently from Soren Kierkegaard. The statement is as follows: "Let the thought of Thee remind us not of what we have committed — but of what Thou didst forgive — not of how we went astray but of how Thou didst save us." With great respect for Kierkegaard, I would amend this to say: "Let the thought of Thee remind us not *only* of what we have committed but of what Thou didst forgive, not *only* of how we went astray but of how Thou didst save us." Those two "not onlys" mean that the statement does not exclude the genuine facing of the negative. It has to be really said — the negative along with the affirmation of "of what Thou didst forgive" and "of what Thou didst save." The forgiving power is there but today we must be sure that the negative is brought to it so that it can be changed.

In conclusion, let us look at two statements from the Gospels. The first is in the Lord's prayer, "Forgive us our sins as we forgive those who sinned against us." It is so concise and full. "Forgive us our sins—as we forgive those who have sinned against us ." It is a prayer when the Presence has been evoked. It starts with "Forgive us our sins," what we have done, where we have alienated people, where we have hurt people. "Forgive us our sins" is in proportion to that which "we have sinned against," or else to the places where we have been hurt. It is not enough just to look at where we are hurt or wounded by the current situation, but it is important that we go back and do deep searching where the original wound took place inside us even though it may seem to be healed. This is the place that Fritz Kunkel called "where you first felt you were killed." Then we can face creative guilt. It is creative guilt to know that we have sinned. It is creative guilt to take on the responsibility of facing it and to know we have been sinned against. It is creative guilt to accept it, and again, in the words of Tillich, to bring the existential anxiety to stay with the Power until it feels accepted.

Then there is the well known incident of Jesus and the

palsied man, and the whole dialogue found there. Jesus says, "Is it easier to say 'Thy sins are forgiven,' or 'Rise, take up thy bed and walk!' "What is he saying? What task do we have there? It is a very simple definition of forgiveness. Forgiveness is the possibility that something can be aroused or constellated through him or through other symbols, which can help me and can help you to do what he says. "Arise take up your bed and walk", take a new direction, don't stay around only in your neurosis. It has always been so interesting to me that Jesus does not say "arise and walk" but "arise, take up your bed, and walk." This is a way to admit the problems are there and to take them along, but not to be completely burdened and overcome by them.

Here then the individual stands, faithful to the wounds, and faithful to the God who is in the wounds, and the hurts and in the healing. There is the wound, the sin and there is healing again and again. But there is growth in it, there is change and transformation through it. In the Navaho creation myth one of the central, the richest divine beings – is called "Wound in the Rainbow". This says that for the Navahos, and perhaps for us, "Wound in the Rainbow" means that there is at the very heart of divinity a sense of incompleteness that needs completeness from us. There is somewhere deep in the heart of existence the most eternal struggle to heal the split between different parts of ourselves, between person and person, between the conscious and the unconscious, between spirit and the substance, the light and dark – the up and the down. If we are aware of this and are committed to this process, then we are working for the process that is God. There is great distress in this and great difficulty but it is also the ultimate meaning of joy. The real process of forgiveness, of being part of this process, this ever growing upward process of facing difficulties, overcoming them — is a tremendous testimony to the Power that is in us as human beings and beyond us. To meet it and go with it is a way to help complete the incompleteness that is in the psyche, in divinity itself and in "Wound in the Rainbow".

CONSCIOUSNESS AND ARTICULATION: THE SIGNIFICANCE OF WORDS AS PART OF THE HEALING PROCESS

Words as tools of consciousness have never needed more to be understood in their creative role and to be analyzed in their negative role than today. In my work as a Jungian analyst and as a leader in the Guild, in my concern for the revitalization of the religious process within theological circles (and seeing the tremendous proliferation of non-verbal groups) I have been extremely involved in this question of the meaning of words and concepts and their role in the healing process.

I would like to share with you some thoughts, suggestive rather than definitive. There are two statements that seem to me basic to my concerns. The first is a part of Navaho Indian religion and myth: "When you name a thing, it becomes." What does it mean to name a thing? What does it mean that "it becomes"? And what was it before it became? This underscores some of the mythological, philosophical background for our thinking. Where was it before it became? What did naming do to it?

The second statement is in Lk. 17:11-19, where ten lepers are healed. Only one of them returns to give thanks and to "glorify God." Jesus says of that one, "You are whole." Why did he say, "You are whole"? They were all healed. All ten were healed, but of only one does Jesus say, "You are whole." Why? What was added by the return to give thanks? What was added consciously? What was added to the physical healing by this articulation?

Words are the great gift of and to man. Obviously they are representative of that high function which distinguishes man from the lower animals. Animals communicate, but they do not use the word. We only have to think of the great literatures of all cultures, East and West, and from all periods of history, to realize how great words can be. And how demonic, as well.

On the evolutionary scale, words are the expressions of

that attempt at consciousness which is man's alone. They are the pangs of unconscious processes to come to birth. I find Sheila Moon's statement, in *A Magic Dwells* provocative and lucid:

> "Beginnings are not precision. Beginnings are not confusion. They are darkness drawn to a minute point of nondarkness, and silence gathered into a small sound."

I like to think about what the first sound that could have been called a word must have been. On the part of man what emotion, what aspect of himself, or what worship, was he expressing?

Religiously and psychologically, words are vessels or containers for archetypal realities. It is as if deep presences within us are putting out feelers into words, longing for manifestation, for expression, for actualization. This is the main thought that I want to begin with, to try to get inside the depths immediately, and to try to see what the depths are wanting, and then to see how words are one of their expressions. This is said poignantly by Rilke the poet, in the *Ninth Duino Elegy*. He says:

> "Are we *here* perhaps just to say: house, bridge, well, gate, jug, fruit tree, window—possibly, pillar, tower . . . but for saying, remember, oh, for such saying as never the Things themselves hoped so intensely to be."

It is always dangerous to analyze a great poet, but is Rilke in some sense echoing the Navaho, asking "Are we here, are we here on earth just to name?" This is in essence the Navaho statement. Man names a thing, a simple, everyday thing of life, because in naming them, they become different—and perhaps we too become different.

Whether, therefore, it is feelings inside us, or thoughts inside us, it is as if these thoughts and these feelings need a creative conceptualization in order for their power to be channeled into the ego for expression. It is as if they need to surface within reach of the ego and its consciousness. And they partly surface through the formation into words. It is as if a framework is present in which the within begins to form, begins to function — a framework that is both imaginatively big enough and realistically limited enough for our everyday living and expression.

Let me return to the Navaho: "When you name a thing, it becomes." Can we say then that inborn realities, "the givens," are there in us, but are waiting for us to name them or to pull them into consciousness for integration? It seems so.

This is to say, of course, that words are symbols, along with many other kinds of symbols. They are symbols and revealers, and they are special kinds of carriers of psychic and divine revelation in the psyche.

Both Buber and Jung have something to say about this. I would like to quote a statement of Martin Buber's:

> "My own belief in revelation . . . does not mean that I believe that finished statements about God were handed down from heaven to earth. Rather it means that the human substance is melted by the spiritual fire which visits it, and there now breaks forth from it a word, a statement . . . a human conception and human speech, which bears witness to Him who stimulated it. Before the word is spoken to man in human language, it is spoken to him in another language from which he has to translate it into human language."

In another place, Buber says:

> "The word has its essence in revelation, its effect in the life of the form."

Jung says in a statement from *Psychology and Religion:*

> "People are not impressed today by the revelation of holiness, but have fallen back on their own mental activity."

And we could select all kinds of statements from the Bible. Here is one from a Psalm:

> "Let your songs be of Him and praise Him, and let your talking be of all His wondrous works."

This is the way it *should* be, if words were really fulfillers of the divine inner—if they were really carrying the revelation from within. But what has happened today? What, in fact, is the contemporary situation? Let us look at it and then let us look at what, if anything, can be done individually to make our own small mark of some change.

Because we are so split from our depths and our psychic realities, we have let words become tools of the intellect and the mind and not of the spirit and the depth. The mind and the intellect today (which is not to belittle either) have become substitutes for the spirit and the depth. Therefore, words are all too often only intellectual expressions of mental activity. Jung has a very telling statement on this — also from *Psychology and Religion:*

> "Our modern consciousness is still on a relatively low level. Nevertheless its development so far has made it emancipated enough to forget its dependence on the unconscious psyche. It is not a little proud of this emancipation, but it overlooks the fact that although it has apparently got rid of the unconscious, it has become the victim of its own verbal concepts.
>
> "Our dependence on words is so strong that a philosophical brand of existentialism had to restore the balance, by pointing to a reality that exists in spite of words. One can be and is just as dependent on words as on the unconscious. Man's advance towards the Logos was a great achievement. But he must pay for it with both a loss of instinct and a loss of reality to the degree that he remains in primitive dependence on mere words.

"Because words are substitutes for things, which, of course, they cannot be, in reality, they become eccentric, outlandish and what schizophrenic patients call 'power words'. The rupture of the link with the unconscious and our submission to the tyranny of words have one great disadvantage. The conscious mind becomes more and more victim of its own discriminating activity. The picture we have of the world gets broken down into countless particulars and the original feeling of unity is lost."

This does not need summary, but is he not saying that in our culture we have become verbal through our cutoffness from the depths, and yet perhaps this has been the inevitable price of advancement? We have become verbal without content and we have become seduced by words, by what Jung calls 'power words,' especially power words in mass media. I think that we are all well aware of that.

Words that were once meaningful and alive have become restricted and sterile, so that when used they express little, and also, perhaps worse, they limit all possible new meaning. Take, for instance, the word "God." For many it has become so virtually sterile due to the attempt to get away from the onesidedly purely transcendental meaning, that a more all-inclusive meaning cannot be reached.

Words that once furnished the living waters because they were inclusive have become frozen, and have in turn frozen the psyche. This, is to say that they have ceased to become symbols, and have become, in Jung's words, "signs." They have become intellectual defenses against real depth, against hearing one another, against genuine relatedness both to ourselves and to others.

Following on this intellectual defense, however, when words, or their instinctive roots, are repressed, then we have overcharged words, as in the phenomenon of the current popularity of four-letter words. The words get loaded because the things which they symbolize have not been accepted enough into the psyche in a natural way. It really is surprising how many people, especially men, but women as well, are much more relaxed in the analytic situation once they have dared to use the four-letter words and I have said them back. Then they can relax. But this is a very deep thing, because it is not just the word that has to be manifest; it is the content. And patients have to know that this is, in fact, acceptable within the analytic framework.

A predictable reaction, it seems to me, to this sterile verbalization, to this purely intellectual use of words, to this fact of words becoming a tool of the intellect or the cheap instinct, and not of the spirit and the depth, has been the tremendous increase of non-verbal encounter groups, which have value but also have some real dangers. It is an historical necessity and a natural swing of the pendulum that we are going through. The positive side is that many people are getting down into the depths, which in our time one cannot always do through the word.

But the danger is *that of having experiences without understanding the experiences*, or that of being psychically hurt by them. Jung says:

> "Interpretation is absolutely necessary before the meaning of a thing can be grasped. The naked facts by themselves mean nothing."

There is always this danger of arousing the unconscious without understanding what it means. And anybody who knows anything about the unconscious knows that it had better not be aroused without some attempt at consciousness. The emphasis in many places on nudity and nude encounter groups may have at its roots some desire to get down to basics but without understanding the *symbolism* of nakedness as a psychic and spiritual reality encountered repeatedly in ancient myths and modern dreams.

I would like in this connection to speak of the work of two professional people in San Francisco, Hildegarde Elsberg and Magda Proskauer, who work with the body.

Hildegarde Elsberg works very closely with people in the Guild, and increasingly is working with the Guild seminars. I think she would say that it is extremely important to *know* when to help a person to verbalize or not to verbalize, in terms of body reaction and body work, whether with an individual or in groups. Far too many people who work with the body have no idea what the archetypes mean, and thus they are, I think, playing with fire. This is not true of the two I mentioned. The mail that comes across my desk every day advertising groups led by untrained people illustrates the kinds of things that are going on. I can't judge them all. I only know that some of them really are kind of horrifying and some of the things I hear about them, too.

If you really understand, as I feel these trained people do, that the psyche does, in fact, live in the body, then you know that you are not dealing with "body" as separate from "psyche." And this is where words, verbalization, conceptualization is extremely important.

Emphasis on the non-verbal can be extremely valuable if it helps lead us, not into more mental verbalization, but into more creative conceptualization from the deep unconscious levels. If we can combine the arousal of the inner with the attempt to creatively conceptualize it, then I think we will be moving forward.

There are many experiences which need not be verbalized, but that does not mean that they need not be conceptualized. I hope that I can make this distinction clear. It is one thing to verbalize something, and it is another thing not to verbalize it but to have your own *logos* conceptual understanding of what it is all about.

Many aesthetic experiences, sexual experiences and religious experiences, are not experiences you talk about all the time. Yet we must have some understanding that is not just either intellectual or some vague undifferentiated emotion. We must understand something of what is being evoked in order to increase our consciousness. Otherwise it passes through and by us.

What then is needed today? What is needed to help to renew—not just the words but the meanings behind them. I am not concerned to save words, but I am concerned to save the psyche, which becomes conscious in part through words. How can we help to renew understanding of the depths in us by the use of creative conceptualization, as I call it, which may or may not always be explicitly verbal but is usually implicitly or tacitly so?

The two fields of which I can speak because I know them most, are the work of analysis and the ways in which the Guild is pioneering. I would like to speak first about Jungian analysis, and *why* words are and *where* words are important in analysis.

It was interesting to try to list to myself the various levels and areas of word importance. The most conspicuous thing about Jungian analysis is that it is usually conducted face to face. Why is it dialogic? Why is it back and forth? So that a new emergent will happen, a new emergent for the patient and, in one sense, something new of value for and in the total situation. Words must be used in analysis and should never become intellectual only. I am not saying that they never do, but they shouldn't,—in the negative sense of the word "mental."

In C. A. Meier's *Ancient Incubation and Modern Psychotherapy* he states that in the Greek Asklepian mysteries the person seeking healing was designated as one who was to be "conversant with the god." This is the truly non-mental religious use of the word.

Why is it necessary for dreams to be written down? I do not know a single analyst who does not emphasize that dreams must be written. Why is this necessary? Why must they not only be vaguely thought about or articulated to yourself, but, in fact, really written down?

Within dreams there is special emphasis when there is a *voice* in the dream. The function of a particular statement by a voice bears usually special attention within a dream, as if the Logos or the spiritual value were trying to say something very definite.

Why is it necessary for a person, even if he feels resistant, to say what he feels, instead of hoping that the analyst will, by some process of osmosis, understand? Once in a while analysts understand and once in a while they don't! But whether they do or not is not the point. The question is, why is it necessary that it be *said*?

A patient once said to me: "because if I say it, I will hear it, and if I hear it, I will know it." This is the best answer I know. (However, often words and articulation are resisted, because one does not really want to know.) This is obviously "know" in the deep sense of knowing, not intellectual knowing. The other reason why a thing has to be said is that if it is said the analyst and all that the analyst represents will also hear it. And because the analyst may be attuned to certain things in the psyche that one is not attuned to yet, one may not want the analyst to hear it because it may mean having to take some new step of consciousness. It is the function of the analyst, in Fritz Kunkel's terms, to be "the lawyer for the unconscious,"– to be not necessarily "ahead" but to come through what I call "the back door,"—to have awareness of unconscious processes, and where they may be leading.

So it is very good to think about why it is important that this tremendous attempt be made to help a person to come through the fog of unconsciousness,– to come into this point of *word* as consciousness, rather than to remain in this vagueness of undifferentiation which can be nothing but a *participation mystique* with one's own inner unconscious and with the analyst.

The other side of the coin is to ask why is it necessary for the analyst to verbalize and to speak to and with the patient? There are many reasons, but analysts help the healing process the most when they do help to verbalize something which perhaps the person cannot yet put into words, and in that sense often the analyst becomes the spokesman for other parts of the psyche. Very often in analysis when you think the patient has not heard something and you often wonder, "Should I have said it?" (and sometimes you should not have said it!) often many weeks later, perhaps even a year later, the patient says, "Oh, that's what you meant," or "That is what was meant when we talked about it earlier." And if it had not been verbalized, it would not have been manifested. That is the best way I can describe the depths that I feel about the meaning of trying to get behind what goes on in words which are used in this most dynamic of all healing processes.

So things do need to be said so that they can be heard. It is a very delicate process, — this process of articulation.

Another field, within analysis, is the whole field of art. There could be places and times where people painting or working with clay have been much too verbal, and therefore it would be very important not to verbalize.

But on the whole, most of us working in the field would be on the side of trying to help the person to articulate. "What in fact does this mean to you?" If this can be done you are a step ahead.

I was working with a woman not long ago who has painted a very great deal in analysis, and has painted creatively, but autonomously. I mean autonomously in the sense that she paints like mad for a while, very dynamically — but often she has had no link with it. Here are these beautiful paintings, but there is no link from the ego to the painting and its symbolic meaning.

I tried to help her to see why it was important that she did articulate whatever the painting meant to her because this is the only way the content of it will get integrated into her consciousness.

There *are* dangers of words in relation to analysis. One of them is saying too soon, outside of analysis, what should be contained within analysis. This, of course, is the wrong use of words, which often ruins the healing opportunity. This is not where words have necessarily become intellectual or cut off, but where the numinous moves into a verbal construct too soon and one has not really lived with it, or where — to use the alchemical symbol —one has taken the lid off too soon, before the inner content is really assimilated.

The other thing about analysis which is very central is that the deeper you go in the inner search, the more important it is really to understand and to be able to conceptualize. This sometimes seems strange to people. I remember Mrs. Jung saying to me "When a person begins to study their animus or anima, then they are really in analysis."

I think "to study," which is the word she used, would mean a real attempt to understand — in my sense of conceptualization — what, in fact, in this case, is the animus, the anima, the shadow, all the different parts of the unconscious. What is it really meaning? What do I need to do about it, with it?

At the beginning, the therapeutic process can be mainly cathartic. One is all excited about all that is emerging of the unconscious. You know it is great—and it is. One is getting at repressed contents, and it is often shocking.

But then one gets down to the nitty-gritty work and that is where one must understand but not as an intellectual construct. Is there really something that grips you? What, in fact, is this journey all about? I am making kind of a plea for the necessity to understand the nature of the journey — not with our heads, not with just words or word constructs, but to really give libido to, or, using Mrs. Jung's term, to study, to understand *how* healing comes about.

The medical analogy holds up and it also does not hold up. Any doctor has to know all the facts he is working with. We, the patients, do not have to know exactly the whole medical thing step by step. But in analysis we do. We don't have to know everything the analyst knows—otherwise we wouldn't be in analysis. But we do have to grasp, as we go along, some understanding of what, in fact, is the nature of the healing process. We have to understand the difference between the personal and the collective unconscious. We have to know what can be learned from myth and legend. Dr. Jung has said that the only thing the analyst has that the patient does not have, is the knowledge of how to read the hieroglyphics. The more intensive we are about the process, the more we have to rely on ourselves in true cooperation with the analyst to learn to know the hieroglyphics. We must be willing to work at understanding with as much of our being as we can. This is central for dream interpretation and dialogue and active imagination.

I would like now to turn to the Guild, and to see what it is doing, which would come under the heading of the creative use of conceptualization and articulation, for the sake of healing and wholeness.

The first thing, of course, is that the very basic structure of the seminars under the Guild is that of articulating the meaning of a text, of amplifying the words — and yet leaving the mystery behind the words as something to be experienced. This is our attempt in all seminars — sometimes successfully achieved, sometimes obviously less so. We are trying to help all of us in the seminar discussion to understand, to experience individually, to be helped by hearing other people and what they have to say, and out of it to come to our own particular experience and understanding of what the statement means to each of us. We are not just talking about nothing. We are always choosing what we think can be numinous material. Dr. Jung has said:

> "Some theologians seem to feel that speculating on ideas like the trinity is simply juggling with ideas."

I want to emphasize that I think anyone (and sometimes one sees this in groups) who thinks that he has ever understood a text completely when he leaves the room, has missed the whole point. This is true most especially of the *Records of the Life of Jesus.* One aim is that we become moved, if we *can* be moved, and that we have a glimpse of understanding. But we must try never to mistake the understanding with the totality of the mystery that is behind the words.

At Four Springs, as in analysis, we use many fields of art where we stress the fact that each person speaks only of his or her own material, and never of each other's. And recently in addition to other aspects of the body work, the impressive work of Ann Davlin has been added in the attempt to implement the meaning of the text with gesture, with bodily expression and mime. We are experimenting with many new things with the help of both Ann Davlin and Hildegard Elsberg. There is a tremendous opportunity for further development in this field in inter-relatedness of verbal and non-verbal approaches. Then there is the whole question of uses of words (in forms of introversion, meditation and prayer) and active imagination. There are also forms of meditation which are, and should be, completely wordless. The important thing is to know which is appropriate for me to be working on in relation to what I need at that time. What part of the psyche is involved? What part of the relationship to the totality of God or of the Self, or of God in the Self do I need to be working with? Many of the great mystics get beyond the use of all words, — in both Eastern and Western traditions. Here again is a field for experimentation for us in the West. Many people are simply afraid to use any words.

Lastly, in terms of the Guild, the very use of the *Records* material itself, is extremely important in this whole area because it is deeply significant to come to a personal understanding of what is behind the experience of two thousand years of Christ as Logos. That is a formulation that has been a genuinely living experience for millions of people. It would not be the way that I would put it or that we would put it. But in studying the *Records*, in studying the meaning of this special life, and the words which this man used, we come to some experience of our own as to what is his contribution, particularly to the struggle for consciousness.

Let me say, in conclusion, that we need to know the limitation of words by knowing all that they do not encompass. But we also need to know the value of words and the value of creative conceptualization in order to help us separate from the vague, undifferentiated experience, of a *participation mystique* inner or outer.

It is not really so much words, or only words, as it is the conceptualization process which in part uses words but which is something intrinsically deeper than the words. I would encourage many of you—not to a more careful use of words that will make you all self-conscious—but to dare to conceptualize more from a feeling-thinking depth and to put into some form, your own inner experiences. There are a great many people who are terribly afraid to articulate or to carve out an understanding which would be helpful to them, let alone to other people. In our own analysis, in our own journals, in our writings, in our own meditations, that instead of fear of using words for fear that it will be a "head trip," why not dare to affirm the creative Logos of discrimination? When we have deep inner experiences, whether in groups, alone, or in therapy, let us bring to it,—even in a groping sort of way—all that we can of genuine understanding, and let us use all the data that come to us, to try continually to change and enlarge our concepts.

We must remember that consciousness does not come from the conscious side. Consciousness comes from the inter-penetration of the conscious and the unconscious. In part, that is what I am stressing here. How can we help consciousness? Words have become identified with the conscious side, in the negative mental sense. If we are trying to help real consciousness to be born from inside, it comes from the interpenetration. Things come from the unconscious. And the conscious ego goes down, in all the various forms that we know, to try to work with these contents.

Returning to the Navaho statement, naming the inner world, in one sense, does not help the inner world to be born. And yet a creative naming is really what I am calling creative conceptualization; that which enables one to have an experience and interpret it correctly, which is a very difficult thing to do.

People are very busy misinterpreting their experiences, and there is often hell to pay for it. They partly misinterpret them to fulfill egocentric needs but they also don't really realize that conceptualization is important.

All of this has, of course, become recognized as important since Jung's discovery of the nature of the personal and the collective unconscious. It is this discovery that has helped us to know the nature of the psyche and the nature of our own central entelechy, the Self. It is not accidental that Jung calls the inner world the *objective* psyche. That is a shock to people when they first discover Jung, because everyone is talking about "Let's be subjective and get inside ourselves." Yes, but it is not just to get inside and wallow around in subjectivity. It is to relate creatively to this objective psyche, which is the given reality—the God given reality. To know what things make what things happen is another way of describing it, not in an intellectual, scientific way, but, "Why did this come out of that?", "Why did working at this dream do this to me?", "Where am I, as I understand the journey?", "What do I need?" It may seem very strange to you that I really am stressing this. I take the risk that some of you can go off now and get all intellectual about this. But I think our journeys are going to be more helped, if we get involved, in what I have tried to describe here.

I am reminded in my talk a short time ago on death and life, life and death, that one of the people with whom the three of us–Luella Sibbald, Sheila Moon and I–had an opportunity to be with at the end, said, "It is meaningful to me to have you- one of you- because you know how to articulate the Source."

Whether true or not, this was a very meaningful statement to me. To know how to articulate not only to a dying person but to ourselves, living, something of wherein the Source is, is extremely important, and how to touch it is the basis of all meaning.

I come back again to the statement from the *Records*, "One returned to give thanks and to glorify God." Could we say that one *of* us, one *in* us, one *part* of us, really knows that to know and to articulate the Source within and beyond, — really means that we would not *identify* with the Source, which we must never do, that we would not remain unconscious of what the deeper Source is doing for us, and also we would not fail in the ultimate humility of acknowledging the grace of God which does come in genuine revelation from within. This would be quite an achievement.

SOME REFLECTIONS ON THE SIGNIFICANCE OF PHYSICAL DEATH IN THE DEATH-REBIRTH MYSTERY CYCLE

What has led me to want to discuss this most mysterious of all subjects, — the relationship of life and death, and death and life, spiritual death and life and its relation to the physical? Dr. Jung has said that "a man should be able to say that he has done his best to form a conception of life after death and to create some image of it, even if he must confess his failure. Not to have done so is a vital loss." Even more specifically, why did this talk come at this time?

I want to express my indebtedness to Barbara Hannah, a Jungian analyst in Zurich, for an excellent article which I read last spring. It is called "The Beyond." This article was the immediate stimulus for this talk, even though it has been stirring in me for quite some time. I shall be quoting Miss Hannah on several occasions, and I owe very much to her and my point of view at some places will be like hers. At some places it will be divergent.

I read Miss Hannah's paper last spring in Santa Fe and Taos where the environment makes one much more deeply rooted in one's Self. Another factor I think, is that I was born on Easter, and I think anyone who is born on Easter probably has a rather special kind of destiny to have to deal with death and rebirth. This has been true for me not only spiritually, but I have also felt that I must deal with the problem of physical death and birth and rebirth.

The most decisive factor, however, has been that I have had the enormous privilege of being with several people who were struggling for consciousness up to the time of their death and to be with them at the moment of their death. This has had an enormous impact on me. It has meant not only having the feeling of my feelings, and the experience of their feelings, but the observation of certain data in those circumstances that have been very impressive and significant.

And also I have been increasingly gripped by the possible negative side of some of the attitudes towards life after death — which, I think, take a great deal of energy from people, which energy could well be spent towards existence here and now. I have debated very deeply how to go at this, because this is not a scholarly presentation. It is not bringing other people's point of view, even those to whom I am the most indebted. After much struggle, this comes as my own point of view. I speak for nobody except myself. I have no desire to convince anybody of anything or to persuade you of anything. If something comes out of this for you in your own thinking or development or experience, that will be adequate. I have a sequence, a development of thought and shall try to say it clearly.

Whether we are speaking of the East or the West, we certainly could all agree that the central meaning of existence, — the central archetype of meaning, — is the archetype of death and rebirth. It is the central meaning in Eastern religion, expressed one way, and it is certainly the central meaning in the teaching of Jesus, and also in the Judaic-Christian tradition, although expressed very differently in all of these traditions.

The process of death and rebirth is, of course, exactly the opposite from the physical sequence of life and death. We speak of life and death because we are born, and we die physically, and then we don't know. The spiritual development is obviously death and rebirth. Death precedes rebirth in the psyche, in the psychological spiritual dimension.

Death and rebirth goes on all the time in us, in nature, in the seasons, in cyclic time. But our problem — our particular problem as human beings — is that we have the choice whether we are voluntarily going to cooperate with that process or resist it. We are the only animal of whom that is true. We have choice, within some limits, whether we will move with this fundamental movement in the universe and in ourselves, or will not. This is the willingness to die in order to find life. We know what happens when we resist it personally. We know what happens in a world where certainly this has not been learned.

And what does this mean more precisely? There are a hundred ways to put it. It means, of course, an everyday attempt of letting go of all the things we are holding onto, — whether we call it ego-centricity, ego-will or ego-direction. It is a letting go of that, to let the new be born — the new outside and the new inside. It is particularly the new inside, — the deep depths in our psyches — that I want to speak of.

This process of death and rebirth is, I think, our fundamental desire, if we only but knew it. And putting it religiously, it is God's desire for us, or the Self's desire, — using the Self, in Jung's sense, as that which is the God-image in each one of us.

Throughout our lives, each of us at our own level needs to be willing "to die and become", in the words of Goethe; "to die and become. Till thou hast learned this, thou art but a dull guest on this dark planet."

In making this conscious, we are going deeper all the time into our own pysches and attempting to come to terms with the unconscious so that we can move more towards the real Self. As Barbara Hannah says, the East speaks of the "subtle body of consciousness" which forms inside us as we come closer and closer to forming our own entelechy. As we come closer to getting free from the purely physical attachments or pure attachment to our ego, and as we go down, and try to find this deeper center which is rooted in the body, we are coming nearer to this subtle body of consciousness, as the abode where the entelechy or where the real Self lives. She goes on to say that this tendency to consciousness builds a kind of subtle body of a spiritual nature, a sort of "mandala like refuge of an enduring kind." This body is made of energy and is only achieved by ways to free this energy, to direct it to the support of the entelechy, that seed which is present from the beginning, the potential, the archetype of wholeness, and it is our work to develop that, to build it a home which is called then "the subtle body."

This is very close to what Erich Neumann would call developing the "mystical man." Some of us may not want to be mystical people, but I suspect in his definition this is what is meant! It is certainly the thing that such a Christian mystic as Angelus Silesius means when he speaks of God being born in us, and we being born in God.

Meister Eckhart, one of the greatest of Christian mystics, has a very beautiful statement. He says:

> "Leave yourself. Remember in this life no one ever left himself so much but he could find something more to leave. Thou goest out of things so much, and just so much, no more or less does God go in. Try it. Though it cost thy all, that way lies true peace and none elsewhere."

I suspect that much of the fear of death has to do with not having actually ever touched or tried to live one's own depths. And I wonder if some of the fear of death would not come under the heading of a really creative guilt that comes because one knows one really has missed the mark, — because one really has not fulfilled the central calling which is the call of this entelechy which is in our potential and which wants us to work with it, to develop it into more wholeness. I don't know what the fear is, but in the people I have known, I suspect a lot of it is that. And perhaps it is good at this moment to remember the parable of Jesus about the eleventh hour. In this parable the workers who come to the vineyard to work towards the end of the day receive the same pay as those who have come earlier. It certainly affirms that the willingness to work is what the Lord requires, and this can be taken as referring to the chronological age as well as more intra-physically. If we begin to work on consciousness even at fairly advanced ages, (I am always very moved when people do just this), perhaps something happens to us.

If it is true that the archetype of death and rebirth is the central reality, and we are attempting, with a sense of committed and creative ego, to move with that, towards more wholeness, may it be then that physical death is the absolutely unique expression of this paradox?

It is in a sense the model, the paradigm. This is the final act, and none of us have been there yet. But it is the ultimate time obviously of going into an unknown without knowing the outcome. This much at least can be said about physical death.

Dr. Herzog, in his book *Psyche and Death* says the death of the past and the painful transformation into the new, "is the constantly recurring process, and the real event of death becomes the symbol of the real event of life, of becoming and transformation." Here at this moment, as far as one can see, being outside it, the ego has to let go willingly, and the question is how graciously and gracefully does it do it. The ego has to detach itself from all worldly concerns, all egocentric patterns for the rebirth to happen.

At this crucial stage, the central entelechy is alive in people or not, depending on how they have lived, — although, again, how do I know? None of us dares judge. Perhaps it comes alive for someone at the last breath. Fritz Kunkel said you can never judge someone until the absolutely last breath. Who knows?

But I would ask you please to think with me, to feel with me, in trying to look creatively at the moment of death, insofar as any of us and all of us are approaching it (Dr. Jung says, we approach it the minute we are born) as a situation which demands the final consummation of the process which hopefully we have been trying to live all of our lives.

In the few people that I have been with, at the moment of their death, in the hours and days of their death, there seems to be an overwhelming evidence for a strong sense of fulfillment, and of trying to achieve final things for wholeness before approaching the end. This is a very important observation to me. In none of the people whom I have known personally was the next life important. They didn't talk about it. I am not saying what they believed, because I wouldn't know exactly. But I would know it was not central.

What was terribly central — and it interested me, it more than interested me, it moved me more than I can possibly say — was the urgency that they had to become all that they could become — whether it was struggling to work through darkness and hostility so that love could be born more deeply, whether it was drawing the circle and the cross just before their death, whether it was the perception of beautiful scenes, whether it was saying "I am ready" as a last statement; there was this sense of preparation. There was no doubt of that.

It was very impressive and very awesome. And of course, the question is, preparation for what? Was it preparation, in their minds, for specific ongoingness? Do these experiences point to something specifically ongoing, *or do they point to the fulfillment of the archetype at the moment of death*, more completely than it ever happened before, or do they point to a beyond? Needless to say I would not know.

But I am going to try to help you to feel a somewhat different approach. As I say, the impressiveness of these people has borne in upon me very, very deeply, partly because towards all of them there was some love, but it was the way that something was moving, and in every case, a tremendous sense of "Why didn't I move with this earlier?"

And that is where I think they can be redemptive for us. Let us listen to them, and let us do all we can. Why did I come to this moment of my end with so much unlived life? We will each approach our death with some unlived life. Of course we will. That is human. But perhaps we can learn something from them and have it be, at least as minimum, a stimulus to make ourselves as whole as we can.

I would like to suggest the possibility that perhaps we project the "life that follows death" into another world, in part at least, perhaps, as a defense against real fulfillment here. All the ideas of reincarnation, immortality, transmigration of souls, may or may not be true. I don't know. But at least I would ask you to be open to ponder with me that some of them contain the numinosity that is put there and could be experienced a bit more here. And that is really my whole desire—to try to make this a bit more real to us. Of course, the pull of the irrational, the pull of the occult, is very deep in all of us and very genuine, but it is also very easy to let it be autonomous and to make theories with it. And I am suggesting that those theories may stand in the way of the living experience, just as creeds and dogmas in the church may stand in the way of living experience. Here again, I am not saying are they true or not. I don't know. But there is a possibility that what we project into them is something that we well might ponder and try to live more deeply here and now. There is a wonderful statement from the Chinese, again quoted by Barbara Hannah, which says:

> "The greatest good fortune which a man can meet is to find a death that crowns his life, — his own specific death."

I think we could be creative and positive about the death that is going to come to any of us, our specific death, not knowing when or how, natural, unnatural, timely, untimely, that crowns his life. I had a very real feeling that for the few people whom I had known, and been with, — that their death was (in a very genuine sense) a crowning of their life. That is a good word; it was putting a crown almost on their life. They had lived vividly. Certainly some of you have known such people. Their meeting of death was the essence of their fulfillment.

If we could for the moment let go of theories and beliefs and could look together and feel more deeply into this subtle body of consciousness — this real Self that has been mine to develop — and to think that we have developed this as deeply as possible, then it will be added to the total body of the struggle for consciousness in the universe that we call God. This is my deepest conviction. What we have attained inside will have meaning to the total reality of the struggle for consciousness. And this Self in me which is different from the Self in you unites us into becoming one together. Please notice that I do not say that we will return to the source or to the stream, because I do not think it is "return" as the leaf returns to earth. I think it is an addition to the ongoingness of life.

What goes back from the subtle body of consciousness is a new creation. It is a new "never before" and "never again" creation, because it has about it the absolute *uniqueness* of the individuality and the personality that each of us develops.

I give back at death what I have received, but I give back what was *in potentia* at birth, and I give it back with whatever development I have worked with during my lifetime. It is like the man in the parable of the talents who takes his money and invests it. And when he goes back to the Lord, he has much more than when he began, as opposed to the man who buried his and didn't come back with anything additional. In fact he lost what he had.

Martin Buber says, "There is no need to have been born if anybody else could ever have been like me." In *To Hallow This Life* he tells this story:

> "This same idea was expressed with even greater pungency by Rabbi Zusya when he said a short time before his death, 'In the world to come I shall not be asked, "Why were you not Moses?" I shall be asked, "Why were you not Zusya?"

Now whether, when this goes back — I say "goes back," that is the only way I know how to describe it, — whether the ego is conscious or not, or has any identity at that moment, after the death of the body, of course, cannot be known. But I feel that our satisfaction cannot depend on it. For myself, it cannot even depend on any belief in it.

What we *do* know is that the achievement of what we

have worked for during our lifetime, will add to the total ongoingness. I believe very deeply with one person who is gone, who said, "Every journey has cosmic significance." That is, of course, a tremendous statement that could be very arrogant and could be divinely humble. I find it a divinely humble statement, because it puts the responsibility exactly where it needs to be, namely, on you and on me — and nowhere else.

Whether or not this reality that is part of the eternal in me and in you, which we work with to develop whether when the body dies and the ego dies this Self has consciousness in the sense of identity, I do not know. I am saying quite honestly that it is not very central to me.

This is very related to another question which we hear people saying often, — "But isn't it all a waste of time if we have had to struggle for consciousness and then we don't go on?" Here is another place of very deep conviction, because this feels to me to be a man-centered question, and not a God-centered question. We ask: "But what about 'little old me?' I have worked awfully hard in this world, with joy, suffering, pain, to become something. What is the value if I don't go on?" But the value is that the very consciousness I have been trying to develop is exactly where I have become part of the eternal flow of things, and this does go on. And this thing in me goes on with it. But for our satisfaction, does it have to go on in the sense that I personally have identity? There again, each one has to decide.

I would suggest that there is absolutely no waste of your life or my life if the aim of our lives has been to help, to form, to enliven, this subtle body, this entelechy, this central reality that is there, *in potentia* at birth, the seed which is waiting for us to do something about it.

We may begin our conscious cooperation with the death-rebirth process because we want life. Jesus makes it clear that "if you enter the narrow gate you find Life." But also, I think we come to know that Life wants to be expressed in us. For it is God's life; it is the greater life.

Of course, we cannot know where the spirit, this Self, this entelechy, goes, except that it becomes part of and I think increases the consciousness of the universe. How it does it, I do not know, but that it does it I know. Teilhard says, "The nucleus of every personality is immortal, and it will retain its uniqueness even in the transformation into the hyperpersonalized state."

One would have to study Teilhard very carefully to know exactly what he means when he says it retains "its uniqueness even in the transformation into the hyperpersonalized state," but I am making, I hope with some clarity, a very subtle distinction between uniqueness and identity.

I think that the Self that each of us develops is unique as well as universal. Whether after death it has identity, in the sense we have thought of as identity, I do not know.

Something goes on. And one could turn the question and say, "What has happened to the infinite through its specific incarnation in me?" Now this is a very bold question, but we must be bold people. It *is* a very bold question to say, "Have I really affected something infinite? If the infinite affects me, have I affected the infinite?"

I think if I haven't, there isn't any point then in the journey. Dr. Jung has written:

> "The feeling for the infinite can be attained only if we are bounded to the utmost. The greatest limitation for man is the Self. It is manifested in the experience 'I am only this.' Our consciousness of our narrow confinement in the Self forms the link to the limitlessness of the unconscious. In such awareness we experience ourselves concurrently as limited and eternal, as both one and the other."

If we experience ourselves as both limited and eternal, is it not probable that the eternal also experiences itself in us, which perhaps is exactly the purpose of creation? To feel that the eternal is affected, that the uniqueness of my tiny fragment of the eternal affects the total eternal uniquely, — this I profoundly believe. Great humility, awesomeness and dignity are added to fruits to be experienced.

There are two other specific points of which I would like to speak before I come to a close. One piece of evidence for what has ordinarily been called life after death, is the sense of the presence of people who have gone. It would be wrong of me not to mention this, because this is a terribly important piece of data. But the question is, what conclusions do we draw from it? And each one again has to find his or her own answer.

That people are very vivid to us, perhaps even more vivid after they have died than before they died in many cases, that people return in dreams, that we can evoke people in dialogue, that we can work, in many cases, at the integration of the values which they have stood for and which therefore we have to work at to get back into ourselves, — this I profoundly know. Nobody here knows this or believes it any more than I do. But I would wonder whether or not this means that they themselves are in person alive. I am sure that they live *for* us, *to* us, *in* us vividly, perhaps over a very long period of time. They may even become more vivid as time goes on. But I am not sure whether we are dealing here with ourselves, our own unconscious, our own symbols, or whether we can say, that because so-and-so is very vivid to me, it necessarily means that the person is alive. That they have made a deep impact on their environment and on me, yes. This much I wanted to say.

Secondly, my whole position of feeling that the working for the uniqueness of our Self and our entelechy, and its attendant deep joy, contributes to the greater Reality and greater Power and that there is no waste if I have been helping that. I also want to affirm the need for greater honoring of ritual and services and ceremonies than most people believe in. This is again part of my own conviction.

We do not honor enough, because of our fear, the final movement of the archetype in this special vessel and we do not honor the *special* vessel after the moment of death. The special vessel may be a very much loved person; therefore there is tremendous poignancy, sadness and grief.

But I think we move away much too quickly instead of hallowing with depths of feeling the meaning of this particular vessel, this particular instrument of God, whatever is going to happen to the spirit afterwards. This spirit has lived in this particular piece of flesh and substance. It has held this spirit, has been the home of this incarnation.

We tend to split it and not to linger enough, from my point of view, with the historical event that has been this person. Certainly in the Catholic tradition the great Requiem masses honor the journey of the person. In other cultures and other periods of history — notably in Egypt — the night-sea journey into the next world has been celebrated by the tremendously elaborate preparations in the tomb for the journey. Is this, in fact, into another world? Is it in fact, in part, a projection? What would happen if we could take it more seriously here and now, — not to cut any of it off, but to be more related to it, with more passion and more urgency in order to have this uniqueness fulfilled.

I am one who believes very deeply that the fact of death, the moment of death, the reality of what one is at the instant, is important. It may not be to you; it is to me, — and if this is my confession, let it be so.

Because of the split in us, because we tend to jump to the spirit, we disparage and forget the vessel, even if we think of the person. The whole tendency today is due in part to a lot of commercialism. The not having services is something which goes deeply against the grain personally.

Where does this all lead us? Again I would like to read to you a statement from Dr. Jung, as I approach closing. He writes:

"You should leave some trace in this world which notifies that you have been here, that something has happened. If nothing happens of this kind, you have not realized yourself, and the germ of life has fallen into a thick layer of air that kept it suspended. It never touched the ground, so it could never produce the plant. If you succeed in completing your entelechy that shoot will then come up from the ground."

I will feel content if I have helped you a little bit to formulate your own understanding of this mystery. Some of you who are very young are not as concerned with it, and yet whether we are young or old, in the kind of world we are in today, we *have* to be somewhat concerned.

It is more natural to become concerned as we get older. But I hope this helps you by agreement — by disagreement — to try to formulate, to try to begin to understand this ultimate of mysteries, — not the fact alone of physical death but the fact of what physical death symbolizes, namely the mystery of death and rebirth. And if it helps you, through formulating it, to fulfill the germ of life and love that has been given to each of us, I shall feel content. If we can know that we have tried, and have added to the ongoingness of the universe, that we have "given notice that we have been here," and that in our very small, limited yet eternal way, we have "notified" both the limited and the eternal side that we have made a mark on them, and that they are altered because of this mark, then this is sufficient.

"THE BEST WAY OUT IS ALWAYS THROUGH"

Each of us stands in the midst of his own life and its evolution. Each of us is part of a world which is evolving. And each of us is part of a country - deeply involved at this particular moment in its creative destiny or its lack of creative destiny. We are part of a fellowship of people working together to foster the ongoing process of evolution - meaning by that the ongoing process of that which makes for meaningful, whole and full living as opposed to destructiveness. What makes the difference between a creature, a culture, a sub-culture or a group which is related to ongoingness and that which is not? The one that evolves is the one that takes the necessary step which is always a risk — is willing to take that risk, that next step from the old form, the old adaptation, the old man, the old community — to the new form, the new adaptation, the new man or the new form of community. Once upon a time a fish said to itself: "I will no longer be willing to be killed or suffocated when the waters recede and the mud comes. I will take a new step. I will develop lungs. I will become a lung fish and I will move to land." And then with this primitive form he chose when he developed lungs to learn how to breathe. He took the next step. Where is the pulse of life pushing us today? Where is the heart beat of evolution pushing us? If we can read this heart beat it seems to be saying that human life at the apex of its genius is striving very desperately for something new against tremendous obstacles and difficulties which may well overcome us before enough of us take the new step. What is the risk and what is this new step?

It is that he, man, shall risk letting go of his own cherished ego images for purposes that are larger than himself, that he shall risk gathering in the scattered fragments of himself, which have been projected outward, and bring them into his own wholeness and substantiality, that he shall risk turning away from his own pre-determined images in relationship to allow the creative flow of the I-thou of any relationship to flow between himself and person or persons, that he shall risk the pride of his group or his nation's achievement for a deeper relatedness to what Teilhard de Chardin called the necessary planetisation *now* of all people, a deeper word for what has been called co-existence. Man must risk some of the apparent certainties of scientific perception for the greater solidity of the artistic vision.

These are some of the ways, and many more could be stated. What does the risk, the challenge, mean to each of us individually and to our work together that there may be ongoingness and life rather than death? In a book on alienation, Gerald Sykes writes, "We must find who we are and what we are doing and then we must place our bets on our most ultimate as well as our most objective discoveries – survival is moral or it is nothing – when we bet in this game we bet everything we have." Before we can see what it is more specifically that we as individuals must do it seems wise to look a few minutes at the contemporary climate in which our lives have to be actualized. We need to see why this next step in evolution is objectively difficult, and that it is not only our perspective that makes it so. Norman Mailer writes, "No matter what the horrors of the twentieth century, the twentieth century is a vastly exciting century – for its tendency is to reduce all of life to its ultimate alternatives." If we can look at it that way, it is exciting to be alive even though at times we may be extremely despairing. The historical shifts which I have seen in the thirty years that I have been concerned with these matters, could be divided into three parts; the shifts and the changes in the physical world, in the psychological world, and in the metaphysical or the spiritual world as it is affected by the first two discoveries, in the physical and in the psychological. These tremendous changes that have gone on and are going on put new questions of who and what is man and who and what is the reality behind the word God, and where and what are the answers. In this lies the radical or the reluctant or the remarkable revolution of which we are a part. For this evolutionary step must be revolutionary if it is to succeed.

In the physical sciences only a few things need be mentioned. At the beginning of my own work, some thirty years ago, the bomb had not been dropped. We each remember the day in 1945 when nuclear power was released for good or bad, for constructiveness or for destructiveness. This brought a whole new insight into the nature of matter, the control of matter and the possibility that through this wonderful and terrible tool the fear of God could be restored to man at a new depth. One aspect of this development has led to the super and supersonic travel, the jet flights, the space flights, the communications satellites — completely altering our idea of space. The whole nature of communication was changed by this change in the time-space continuum. The moon-landings have exemplified the negative reach of technological man, at the same time expressing his desire to reach a mystery beyond himself. Also, the growth of ecological awareness has come to the forefront of man's attention, as a product of his unconsciousness about the matter of the universe which he suddenly finds he is destroying.

Another result in the technological area is the growth of computer systems — on the one hand giving man leisure, which perhaps he does not know how to use — and on the other hand de-personalizing and mechanizing man and challenging him as to whether he will become a high class robot who programs lower class robots or whether he will really develop his own absolute uniqueness. In the medical sphere there is population explosion, the possibility of longer life, the fact of birth control, the pill, and the whole moral problem which is presented because of this. The whole field of sexual morality is shifting from an outer authoritarian to a deep inner personal challenge. Man has become or can now become mechanistic, determined, impersonal, or he can move ahead to the greatest fulfillment that he has ever had. Teilhard writes, "Actually we are just now beginning to feel the immensity of our universe and the coalescence of mankind, and these two pressures are the cause of the fear and trembling which we all experience . . . we are at a critical point – the point where humanity passes from divergence to convergence, or perhaps one should say at the point at which mankind can pass from divergence to convergence."

In the field of psychology and its philosophical

implications, two great movements are in process — the knowledge and expansion of the field of the analytical psychology of Dr. Jung and the field of existentialism. Analytical Psychology began with Jung's break with Freud. Almost every year now, the influence of Jung particularly on culture, on history, art, and education is becoming greater. Most of you are aware of the main realities and concepts which Dr. Jung particularly has emphasized, and which are empirically, pragmatically based. Jung has changed our attitude toward the inner depth, the tremendous reservoir in the human psyche, which Freud began to discover. In that great reservoir, in that creative depth in everyone, is to be found the dark element that Jung points out we have neglected — the deep feminine element whether we are men or women, and sorely needed in the world today. The central element which he calls the Self is the core of our being which has about it a deep intentionality. Not only in matter outside, but in substance inside there is purposiveness; there is intentionality; there is movement, a movement teleologically towards something. We, the conscious side, have the freedom to move with it or to move against it. This discovery of the Self, beyond the ego, has changed our concept of the nature of man and our concept of the reality behind the word God — has enormously changed it. It has put the possibility of what he calls the God-image in the Self — therefore within man. It has put a responsibility on man for his own choices. It has made man responsible for whether he does or does not explore his own depth and it has certainly done something very central to that which is moving in the universe. This something behind the word God is no longer only out there; it is also deeply within. The whole implication of the discovery of the way the unconscious works, the mythological element, changes the inner dimensions of space-time, as nuclear physics has explored the outer dimension of space-time.

In the scientific field the irrational as well as the rational is being included. Cause-and-effect is being supplemented by the concept of Synchronicity. The microphysical world as well as the macrophysical world of astronomy is having to give up completely old-fashioned causality in favor of an approach where Synchronicity more inclusively "explains" whether electrons behave as particles, or waves, or wavicles.

The purposiveness Jung found in the psyche, science is just now coming to see — i.e. admitting that reality shows intentionality behind it in very irrational ways. All the scientific research going into areas such as drugs, REM sleep, E.S.P., shows that science is now exploring irrational areas, as if to balance the overly "robot" object.

Not exactly parallel time-wise and yet not completely unrelated to it is the emphasis of the existential movement — whether it is religious existentialism or non-religious existentialism. The tremendous value of this is that it is asking the right questions about the *here and now;* it is asking questions about how am I engaged with life. How am I encountering life. How am I confronting life. Am I really in a dynamic relationship to my situation or do I tend to stay aloof from it? The non-religious existentialists and the religious existentialists will answer that question differently — the difference being the attempt to *make* meaning versus the attempt to *find* a given meaning. But it is extremely interesting that both analytical psychology and existentialism have appeared somewhat parallel and at this time as if both of them involved a tremendous critique of the Church among other things. Here "church" is used in the broadest sense — not any one sect, not Catholicism, Protestantism, or Judaism. Much of the concern with the nature of human nature and practical existence has had to develop outside the church. It has represented a very deep need of the human soul to be concerned both about its own depths once again and to be concerned about its encountering and its engagement and its dialogue with the other.

The whole field of religion and theology are very deeply affected by these developments in the physical and psychological sciences. From the despair that showed itself after the world wars and an eschatology of other-worldliness it seems that now there is emerging a new religious hope of immanence that is not only humanistic but is based on a realizable transcendence as found in the works of Teilhard, Tillich and Jung. It is based on the new discovery of space and time through the physical sciences and through Teilhard's emphasis on the thrust to consciousness of pattern and meaning in all things. And it is based on the discovery of the realities of the deep inner world, which Tillich calls the "Ground of Being" and which Jung speaks of as "intentionality in the psyche". This shift moves the emphasis to the within and to the necessity of the within being expressed *in the moment.* It gives a whole new look to the rather exciting controversy called "Is God Dead?" If one looks at this shift of meaning and how the search for meaning is changing, then the answer comes: the concepts, images, symbols are changing. Behind the symbols the Christian God *is* dead, but that is not to say God is dead. The question, especially for the theologians, is whether they get attuned to the changes. The whole field of religion is being challenged and influenced by the mythological emphasis, by the understanding of symbols. Robinson's book *Honest To God* reflected this, and so does all the subsequent discussion. An understanding of the nature of the symbolic process in the psyche, of personal and collective myth, helps us to understand how and out of what all the stereotyped dogmas and creeds originally developed. If we can get back to the *living* experience then there is hope; if we get stuck in the static attempt to *believe* something then nothing happens. Dr. Jung once said, "If one *knows*, one doesn't have to believe." The task today is to *know* with our whole being.

Also in the field of religion and metaphysics, the whole East-West interpretation is most significant. I cannot speak with any authority about the East, but I can say something about what is happening here, in regard to both negative and positive influences. The negative side seems to be that sometimes people have tried to substitute the eastern way for the western way, and Dr. Jung says we dare not do that but that instead we must develop our own western techniques. The positive side is that many opposites are presented from the East and it is challenging to the Judaic-Christian tradition to find a much deeper value in its own tradition.

The whole ecumenical movement has tremendous implication in terms of the growth towards convergence instead of divergence. There is in recent years a great deal of emphasis once again upon the Gospels and on the life and meaning of Jesus, including the mythological element. All the archaeological discoveries, revealed particularly by the Dead Sea Scrolls and their influence on religious concepts, have happened within these years. There is the area of folk music and lyrics. If one reads all the words of some of Bob Dylan's songs one finds the religious emphasis. And among the "top ten" most popular songs a great deal is being sung about Jesus, and it is wonderful to hear Joan Baez, Judy Collins and various rock groups sing them. The new rock opera *Jesus Christ, Superstar* is one more piece of evidence.

The whole contemporary climate demands that we see the dignity, the new dignity and the terrible responsibility that now belongs to man as against almost over-whelming impersonality and the emphasis towards irresponsibility. We must face that, outer and inner, there is that which makes for meaning, that which makes for wholeness, that which makes for integration, that something is at work, whatever name we give to it, and I say the question that confronts us is: do we stand with what is at work or do we stand against it?

This contemporary climate which we have glimpsed shapes the moments of our lives, for each man stands in the midst of each of the moments of his life. What is the shape and what is contained in any moment of our life — both from the viewpoint of the eternal and from the viewpoint of the temporal? At any one moment, if we stop to analyze it, there are three elements present: there is first of all "I", the person — "I" with the possibility of the affirmation of freedom; secondly there is the impingement of all the outer events at any moment — the situation, the circumstance, fate, if you will. Thirdly there are all the inner factors — all the things which are coming from within the psyche which impinge on the conscious side. I want to discuss four ways in which we approach life and the moments of our lives. Every moment has in it these facts:

the person — the events from outside and the events of inside — but *also* from both outside and inside there is a spirit working — a self — a purposiveness which is "breathing" through the facts and which is confronting us. In the words of Kierkegaard it is that which is cross-examining us. *I* cross examine the moments of my life, but also the situation in which I am, if I am open to it, cross-examines me; it asks me a question. I am continually being asked a question by the nature of my inner self, and I am being asked a question by the nature of that which is outside of me. If this is the nature of moments which make up the continuum of my life there are four ways in which I meet the moments of my life, the situations of my life. Three of them are negative and one positive. The last one is what I am most concerned with. The four ways I will call the *Great Evasion*, The *Great Split*, The *Great Immersion*, and the *Great Emergence.* And "The best way out is always through" is this fourth way.

The *first* way — the Great Evasion — is the way of the collective, and none of us dares say that we are completely free from it. It probably is the obvious way in which most people are caught. We who have some insight pride ourselves that we are not as caught in it as most people are. Probably the second and third ways are the ones which would touch us more personally. But the first, The Great Evasion, is the turning back from the challenge of life at almost every moment; it is turning back from the moment. It is isolating oneself from the moment. It is giving no feeling response to the moment. It is making a conforming adjustment to the moment — and an adjustment always means that there is no real dynamic response. It is this which pervades our society and our country to a devastating degree. Why do we do this? Why do we turn back? What are we afraid of? In a very impersonal world, in a world that praises what our culture praises, we are afraid of involvement and responsibility. We are afraid of emotional and feeling responses. We are afraid that if we are involved then our old ego-centric patterns will be done away with. So we remain isolated in our own little ego-centric castles and we manipulate life. What happens to us then as people and what happens to the situation which we do not really enter into? Out of this kind of attitude there is a crystallization into the secular establishment, into the status quo, into the whole power system. If we do not really confront situations, then we freeze. We freeze into a mass of prejudices, of fixed patterns and of defensive mechanisms. Our anxiety and our guilt grow because we have left unfulfilled our real natures, and what we have *not* met becomes more frozen, rigid, static and stereotyped. In one sense, for the person with this attitude of turning back, there is really never any real moment of encounter or of dialogue; because there really is never a *person* present. Every one of us at some time has been caught in this. There is in it a self-perpetuating sterility. Nothing moves forward. I do not move forward, I do not help the ongoingness of values, I do not help the ongoingness of meaning in the world, or of God. Mark Pelgrin in his book *And A Time to Die* says,"It is only the man who has turned his back on life that excludes himself from continuous creation of the universe." The universe is in continuous creation; life is in continuous creation inside us. We in our encounter could be in this creation but we turn our back on it, and so we and life become frozen and static.

The *second* way I call the Great Split. It is the closest of the four to what I think has been the Christian problem, in the broad sense. In this, there is action, there is spirit, there is ego involvement, but there is one-sidedness because the movement forward is with only part of the self, or part of what is observed or faced, and *not* with the whole. If one were to diagram these first two ways, the first would be a moving back and the second one would be a forward movement but to the right and not through the center. There is here a tremendous, emphatic, spiritual urge, sometimes with great stoicism and very real discipline which must not be belittled. But it has left out much of what is in the center and to the left which is of the substance - the hidden, the more feminine inner depth side. This is part of the crisis of the church and what Dr. Jung helps us to see. Why this split? Why has the whole not been faced? Perhaps there have been natural historical reasons but which also have been dangerous. In the statement of the two Commandments: "Love the lord thy God with all thy heart, soul, strength, and mind, and thy neighbor as thyself" — the way of the split has been to try to love God and the neighbor but not the Self, and this has been the tragedy. The Self has been put over here aside, and the third way which I will discuss in a minute deals with this. But in the second way there is tremendous value, there is dialogue, there is encounter — but it is not really holy because it is not whole. It is partial, and what happens then? Here a religious system comes into formation that tends to be authoritarian, with a real danger of hypocrisy. The autonomous reactions of the unconscious stay unexpressed, and out of them repressions, guilt, anxiety and explosions occur. So in this picture of the Great Split, there is motion and movement; but it is not of the whole. Somehow the action is a detour. It does not go through the totality — either of the psyche or of the total reality of the situation.

The *third* way I call the Great Immersion, and it is one of the most important to talk about today because it is in a sense the newest. It is the great danger of getting lost in the lure of the inner. One form this takes is all the acting out of all of the anti-social behaviour and anti-social rebellion which is a kind of getting lost in the unconscious. But the kind that I am particularly concerned with is the danger of getting lost in the unconscious rather than in working with it, bringing it to consciousness and moving through it. This emphasis is very natural, and in part a creative and positive compensatory reaction to the second approach. It comes out of a tremendous hunger-as-longing for depth and for contact between people. Under this heading I would put certain forms of mysticism, the phenomenon of glossalalia, the chemical cushion of the hallucinatory drugs, some forms of group work and even perhaps some forms of analysis. All of these may have tremendously positive results for the moment; they may even produce a pseudo-revelation and a sporadic creativity. Two things that Paul Tillich said have impressed me. When he was asked a question about the use of drugs, he said, "They bypass the most essential aspect of man - which is freedom of will". And, "Instead of making one's own decision the forces of the unconscious may be accepted as oracular." This is an extremely important thing to be clear on. This is a natural development, an exciting possibility, as already said, but also a tremendous danger. The only reason for going inside ourselves – the only reason for coming to know our unconscious, is so we may become more of a real person, a real human being. The danger of any short cut is the danger of wanting to do it the easy way, and the deceptive thing is that it seems to happen in this kind of experience. In these experiences one tends to feel one is in the moment, but actually one is lost to the moment, for the ego is overcome. The danger of moving into and being immersed in the unconscious is the danger that the moment really does *not* get born—the moment itself. It, the moment, remains shapeless, because in this sporadic creativity there is not necessarily an ongoingness to the creativity of becoming a human being. The really great art form of life is that art form by which we are to attain human beingness. There is great potential here, but the danger is that the ego is wiped out for the moment, and there is no real life achieved except through the relation of the conscious or the ego to that which is discovered within the depths.

And now I come to the last—the *fourth* way, the Great Emergence—"The best way out is always through" which is a line from a poem of Robert Frost. In the Great Emergence—the positive way—there is the attitude not of going back, not of going to the side and evading, not going in with the danger of being lost by the tremendous inner power. Rather it is the attitude of affirmation, of facing that which is inside and that which is in the situation, engaging with that which one encounters from inside and outside, engaging with it decisively and courageously. As Tillich says, with all the "in spite of—all the obstacles," all the difficulties, the conflicts, the hostilities, there is the affirmation to go ahead. This is the all-inclusive attitude of working at knowing oneself, slowly, encountering that which is to be encountered each moment. It means taking on oneself what Tillich calls existential guilt, the anxiety of guilt, and using it creatively. This effort – and the affirmation has to be re-affirmed over and over again—

helps one to become what one is originally supposed to have become. Whether one puts it archetypally, psychologically or religiously there is in each one of us that which is meant to be one's most unique self, the God-given potential which helps us to affirm. This means opening oneself to one's own depth. It means opening oneself to the shape of any moment, and the moment may be very distorted, it may be very beautiful; a very fun moment, a gay moment, or a very serious moment, a moment of sorrow, a moment of grief. But it means, no matter what it is, facing it. It means somehow going through it, encountering it, working with it. What happens out of this kind of encounter from the within and from the without is that both the person and the moment then are changed, and this is the "out" that is the step of emergence in a true evolutionary sense. This means facing our abyss. From the standpoint of the moment, when the person responds and attends to manifestation, then the pregnant value in the moment gets born. Every moment has about it a value that is waiting, but it is waiting for a man, or a person. It is waiting, it is waiting for me, and what am I doing about it? I think this way includes God, the self and the neighbor.

The first way, the Great Evasion, really does not include any of the three. The second way, the Great Split, is the emphasis upon God and neighbor with the danger of omitting the Self. The third way, the Great Immersion, is the danger of the new excitement of finding the Self, of getting immersed in it, without really manifesting it in total meaning or in relation to the neighbor. I think this last way, the Great Emergence, includes all parts. Here the value or new consciousness is realized and this then would be the help to the ongoingness of values. For the person who does this it is certainly a way of joy, a way of hardship, of discipline, but a way of joy because it is the way in which one can really feel inside oneself that one is at least attempting to fulfill the given. This is also the way by which real revelation comes about. Marya Mannes in a recent article said, "and why do you need drugs to give you excitement and revelation when the real world if you really bother to examine it is so full of both." Not only the real world but also the real inner world is so terribly full of exciting, wonderful, difficult but moving things if only we would take the patience and the time to be aware of it. The fourth way is a way by which love is born, not only as a sporadic experience, not only as something that just happens but as something that one can really work at, to manifest the continual commitment to the way of love. Affirmation means the love of life — the love of the totality of meaning; it means to love all of one's parts good and bad, dark and light. It means loving the birth process itself. It means being willing to create and re-create. Finally it means, in the words of Arnold Toynbee, "In time of troubles individuals turn from the outer world of political and social chaos to the inner world of the psyche. There they come upon the vision of a new way of life and return to the outer world to form the nucleus of a creative minority through which civilization may find renewal." The fourth way, then, is the one in which we have to go inside but also is the way by which we become part of a creative minority who come back and try to do something in the real world.

In conclusion let me turn to the opening line quoted in a writing of Jung's from the Timaeus of Plato which says, "One, two, three but where is the fourth?" I would like to re-phrase it - "one, two, three but where, O where is the fourth . . . ?" There is a cry in the universe today calling to those who will face the hero's path within to find their journey and to go on it as the fourth way. There is a cry in each of our own hearts to answer that cry behind all of our defenses. If we put these two cries together—the cry from the universe and the cry from inside ourselves—and dare to stop long enough to listen, then I think they spell, in the words of Nikos Kazantzakis, action and "holy action". This is concern for wholeness at all levels. This is the crucial need today.

THE FORGOTTEN FEMININE IN THE GOSPELS

What is the "feminine"? Why is it urgent and imperative to talk about the feminine, especially the forgotten feminine today? Because never has the feminine been more needed than it is now, and because our Christian symbolism has on the whole lacked it. Let me say at once that by feminine I do not mean woman. The feminine principle (The Eros as defined by Dr. Jung) is that which accepts, that which is inclusive, which binds, which heals, which relates things one to another. In our western world we tend to talk *about* things rather than to get into a dialogue with them, into relationship with them. It is imperative that we not only think about but that we feel into this principle of relatedness, because out of it comes the whole possibility not only for our personal lives but also for the coexistence or co-inherence in the larger world. Most of our current culture, whether sacred or secular, is dominated by the masculine principle, the scientific, the technological. The growing thrust of the women's liberation groups is a counter-movement against this domination by the masculine principle. Much of their concern is positive and is influencing various aspects of the culture. Nonetheless, it could be important for women's liberation groups to remember that when they discard the feminine principle, calling it "weak", "passive", "submissive", etc., they are "throwing out the baby with the bathwater". They, too, are rejecting the feminine principle and too often using masculine principle thrusts when the opposite would achieve their commendable ends much better. Both masculine and feminine principles need to be used equally—and few have done so for thousands of years. Not even women's liberation. Such a relationship is beautifully stated in Eccles. 24:9, where Wisdom (feminine) speaks, saying, "He created me from the beginning—before the world—and I shall never cease." So it is very important to stress the feminine as opposite, and if one looks at the trends in religion and theology today, there are evidences of an emphasis on substance, on the irrational, and on eros as relatedness. The emphasis of Paul Tillich upon the "Ground of Being", the need to go down and inward is relevant. Tillich sees the need for self-affirmation as being the expression of God, and when he states in *The Courage to Be* that "the courage to affirm oneself must include the courage to affirm one's own demonic depth", this means going into the dark, unknown regions of one's substance.

Major emphasis on encounter in religious existentialism is apparent in the contribution of Martin Buber with his "I-Thou" versus the "I-It". This same stress, in different language, is very prominent in the works of Teilhard de Chardin, with his emphasis on the continuity of evolution and the presence of spirit within matter. Thus in the Protestant, Jewish and Catholic traditions there are new emphases stirring. The contribution of Jung is that of the person and scholar who helps us understand what the feminine actually is *within* ourselves and how we can relate to it, so it may be brought into our total existence and religious way of life.

It occurred to me after I chose it, that this title could have been "The Forgotten Feminine in the Forgotten Gospels", because the Synoptic Gospels have, on the whole, been the forgotten Gospels of Christianity. Christianity has mainly been concerned with the religion *about* Jesus as found in the Gospel of John and the letters of Paul. The living words of Jesus become pre-Christian, and yet, perhaps if we go back to what is pre-Christian we will be ready to face the next era - that of the post-Christian world. I am not stressing the historical Jesus demythologized, as in the work of Bultman, and I am not talking about Liberal Protestantism. I am talking about certain movements, trends, archetypes, especially the feminine one, which I believe Jesus himself manifested and exemplified. In looking at the gospels this way we may get help for ourselves, insight into the deeper archetype for our own lives to make them more relevant and even more living.

When we turn to the Synoptic Gospels we may find the manifested feminine principle symbolized in three different areas. First, in the nature of the Godhead, the Divine, the great Thou, that which is more than ourselves, inside and outside, which endows our life with meaning, and which expresses the thrust of evolution. Secondly, we see it symbolized in man himself as a reflection of the Divine, in certain attitudes that can be expressed in actions as well as in figures of women. And thirdly, there is the feminine principle as expressed and manifested in the central Journey to wholeness, in the transformation process itself. Separately we may also see how Jesus himself incorporated that principle through his experience, and how he manifested it in his life, and what happened to it after his death that led to Christianity, that is via the post-crucifixion events.

First let us look at the feminine symbols in the nature of the Godhead, or at least in our image of it. The most conspicuous expression of the feminine dimension is in the nature symbols which one finds in abundance within the Gospels. There is much emphasis upon substance, upon nature, and upon symbols such as earth, ground, leaven, vineyard, the body, the seed. This is parallel to what Eric Neumann in his book, *The Great Mother*, calls the "elementary" level of the feminine principle. There is the emphasis upon patience and upon letting things happen in the ground through germination. The parable of the wheat and the tares (Mt. 13:24) says, "Do not separate them too quickly." The nature principle is there waiting to be transformed.

Another attribute of the Divine is the emphasis upon "all-inclusiveness" versus "perfection". In the passage on letting the rain fall on the just and the unjust, and the sun to shine on the evil and the good there is another text in which it reads, not "Be perfect as your heavenly Father is perfect," but, "Be ye all inclusive." (Mt. 5:48) As Jung pointed out, perfection is a masculine principle and all-inclusiveness is a feminine principle. This attribute of all-inclusiveness we very much need today because we are dominated by negative judgments and by harsh projections which stand in the way of our being able to relate authentically. There are also some passages which very much confirm the aspect of the spirit which is intrinsic to substance, the aspect stressed in the thought of Teilhard de Chardin as the Omega within, and what Eric Neumann calls the transformative principle within. The statement of

Jesus, "The Kingdom of God is within . . . ," implies that that which is within the psyche has spirit within it, which has the possibility of transformation. Today this is not a heretically radical statement. Two thousand years ago it was, and it could not be accepted at that time by Jesus' own people. It is a very great thing to realize that there is something of divinity and of potentiality within the psyche (which Dr. Jung has called the Self).

There is a parable, following the Lord's Prayer, on importunity (Lk. 11:5). In this parable a man comes from a far journey at midnight to a friend, asking for bread. The friend has none but he goes to another friend who has bread but is asleep. He, the one with the bread, must be awakened by persistent effort. This happens and the bread is given. One sees here the sleeping, passive God who has the bread to give to the one who needs it, but who must be aroused. It is urgent that God as Substance, or God-substance within, be aroused by the individual ego. He-She has the possibility of giving the food which makes for wholeness and for growth, but there has to be activity on the part of the human being before it can be obtained. Not only is the feminine principle seen here in the sleeping God but also in the fact that it is midnight, and nadir of Logos, Sun, the masculine principle.

We turn now to the *second* category, the feminine in the human as a reflection of the Godhead. This category can be viewed in four parts. One is in Jesus' picture and image of man's nature. How did he see man? Was he a realist or was he not? Second, we see his emphasis upon inwardness and incubation and containment. Third is his emphasis upon relatedness and love or eros. Fourth, is his emphasis on compassion and feeling or agape.

Jesus' insight into human nature is that of a man who was a tremendous realist. Let us look at certain passages. Jesus emphasized the fact that we must face anger when it is there and work for transformation (Mt. 3:23). He says that lust is there and not to be condemned, but to be dealt with in new ways (Mt. 5:28). We see the way he deals with egocentricity. If one looks at the "woes" in the discourse to the scribes and Pharisees, he harshly points out how man tends to all the smaller matters rather than the weightier things of the law (Mt. 23:13). He emphasizes that when we cast out the devil he wanders around and may come back many times worse again! (Lk. 11:24) This is a man, then, who knew man in his unredeemed state and was urgently concerned with the one question of how man can change. Look at one of his central teachings which has been so often misunderstood, "resist not evil." (Mt. 5:39) He does not say "resist evil," which would be a negative masculine attitude; he does not say "give in to evil," which would be a negative feminine; rather he says evil exists. We resist outer evil in the wrong way because we have resisted it inside; we have repressed it and projected it instead of dealing with it. Dr. Jung has emphasized in *The Undiscovered Self* that one thing which we lack today is "imagination in evil", because we have no idea how bad we good people are! Jesus shows his relation to the feminine principle in the way he talks about the relation to the law. He stresses certainly the law on the masculine side, the mosaic patriarchal law, but he also shows what must be the basis of decision – when one is criticized for not always obeying the law. Here he stressed that the demands of substance must take precedence over the law. "Look at your predecessor David; he put his need first." The needs of man, the needs of his substance, the reality of human nature: this is what this man was concerned with. Here was the Judaic law, but as against it he always put the other side with the emphasis on mercy and love. And he says, "The Sabbath was made for man, not man for the Sabbath." (Mk. 2:27)

Secondly, there are many passages which show his emphasis on inwardness and on containment. One of the most striking instances is in the Sermon on the Mount where he says, "Do not your righteousness before men, but rather do your almsgiving, your praying and fasting in secret, that your Father which seeth in secret may recompense thee." (Mt. 6:2-6; 16) Here the emphasis is on the introverted, inner attitude, and not on the extravert, flamboyant side, or that which can lead to outer rewards. A similar emphasis is found in the passage previously referred to: "If you find at the altar that you have anger against your brother go and work with it." (Mt. 5:23) He does not say forget it; he does not say express it. He says go work towards reconciliation. This is a third way, not repression or direct expression. It contains the possibility of confronting the brother, whether an actual person or an inner psychic content (the shadow) and working with him until a new relationship is found. Anger dealt with in this way, keeping the Presence received from the altar always before one, has a chance to turn into integration and love and the healthy expression of the transformed negative. The whole scene in the wilderness (Mt:4:1-11,Lk. 4:1-13) after the baptism may be seen as being one of incubation and of containment. He goes to the wilderness after the baptism to ask what to do about this experience—what to do with the power he has received, and he works and he struggles for a long time to know where to express it, what to do about it, and he comes up with a radical individual answer.

The third aspect of feminine attitudes within man is Jesus' emphasis upon the eros principle — the emphasis upon feeling and relatedness as a component within the self. In modern terms this is Buber's emphasis on the "I-Thou" versus "I-It," the asking the "who" rather than asking about the "what." There are many aspects and many parables that show this, but none is more beautifully stated than that of the Good Samaritan. (Lk. 10:30) Here is the wounded man, the beaten man, the man who has suffered evil, the man inside us who has suffered from outer hostility and inner hostility, and also he is suffering mankind. The Priest and the Levite pay no attention to this man, whether outside or inside. Because these respectable, conforming, more orthodox religious aspects of ourselves are busy about their own goals, the wounds are untended. It is the Samaritan, the rejected outsider, the outcast, who acts with compassion. He sees the suffering; he responds; he takes the man, puts him on the horse, takes him to the inn, offers to give and to pay more than is really necessary. He goes far beyond the call of duty. Here is gentleness; here is relatedness; here really is love. Of course the question is how do we find or develop this

Samaritan inside ourselves! The genius of Jesus in part lay in the relatedness quality in his teaching. His teaching was never divorced from reality; it was never abstract; it was never concerned with only theological speculation; it was not concerned with belief but was concerned with experience. It was concerned with masculine law and existential resurrection now. It was a beautiful combination of masculine and feminine.

The fourth quality under the aspect and attitudes in man that reflect the feminine part of the Godhead is that of poignancy and compassion, as agape. One of the deeply stirring statements of the feminine feeling comes when Jesus is looking at his city in the last days of his life, "Oh Jerusalem, Jerusalem which killeth the prophets and stoneth them, how often I would have gathered thy children together as a hen gathers her own brood." (Lk. 13:34) If there is any image that is of a really feminine quality it is certainly that of the brooding hen. It is as if he is saying, "I loved you but you will not respond to me." There is nothing sentimental here but there is a great sense of poignant feeling.

There is the incident of the woman of the city streets, the great silent dialogue between her and Jesus. (Lk. 7:36) She comes to him with tears and oil; she comes with openness to respond to the new value which she has just perceived, although rejected by the Pharisee host. She comes with repentence for the misuse of her powers. She has the ultimate courage of which Tillich speaks, when he says that "the greatest courage is to accept acceptance." This Jesus could give her because of what he had learned of repentance and acceptance at the baptism. She is the free giving, prodigal side in us — spending itself in wrong directions. Perhaps we do not achieve more spiritual transformation because we condemn her as did the host, and so she has little chance in us. Also, the Pharisee in us is warmed by so little love because he — unlike this woman, will not admit his need for forgiveness and to forgive. Jesus' dialogue with her is his absolute acceptance rather than any judgment of her, and his words "Thy faith has saved thee" exemplifies his attitude. It is one of the most creative dialogues to be internalized inside any one of us - to help us in the transformation of this dark side from the misuse of power to focused power and to define genuine forgiveness.

The third category is that of how the feminine is shown in stories having to do with the total transformation process, with the Journey itself from the first natural birth to the second birth. The two incidents I have picked out here are those of the prodigal son (Lk. 15:11) and the storm at sea. (Mk. 4:35) In the story of the prodigal son there are several significant feminine symbols. It is perhaps closest to the mythologem which Jung calls the "night sea journey," or the descent-and-return cycle. In the story, the younger son, after he asks for and is given his substance, journeys to the far off land, eventually falling into the deepest abyss where he is reduced to tending the swine. The pig belongs to the oldest godesses and are to be found in most of the Greek mysteries. This very ancient symbol is frequently connected to the descent to a divine earth mother. But he comes to him*self* - perhaps the self that Jung means - and returns then to serve the Father. This is the discovery of the self within substance, out of his descent. This is to find the spirit within matter, so when he returns, the father welcomes him with an eternal feeling quality. Compare this with Demeter weeping over the return of Kore from the underworld. The compassion, the fact that the father greets him with a kiss, the change in the father, is surely interrelated with the experience of the son. This parable is a presentation by Jesus of a new way to conceive of the Godhead and of interaction during the man's journey to himself.

The next incident is that of the storm at sea. (Mk. 4:35) The disciples and Jesus are crossing the Sea of Galilee in a boat when a storm arises. Jesus is asleep, the disciples anxiety-filled. In their need they awaken Jesus, and soon the storm quiets down. There are many levels of interpretation. Strong storms arise and subside quickly on inland waters such as the Lake of Gennesaret. These were fishermen that knew their lake, but did Jesus' wakeful presence carry too much assurance? There are other interpretations. But let us see it symbolically. The water symbolizes the great unconscious feminine depths and the storm is raised by the spirit. The boat itself is a vessel, a container, which relates us to the depth with some security. (I remember a very old picture in a Jerusalem church which portrayed Jesus and the disciples in the boat, and the boat itself is a woman.) In the story, Jesus himself is asleep, relaxed at the bottom of the boat. He is well related to the feminine. The disciples are afraid. They are overcome by the storm. And their need is to awaken him who carries the value for them.

What was the origin of the emphasis and the manifestation of the feminine in the experience of Jesus? The baptism was the experience of Jesus which coincided with a synchronous movement of the archetype in evolutionary history. The whole God-man relationship moved more inwardly, and Jesus manifested the new movement. The first feminine symbol in this experience is not an ascent but a descent into water, which Christianity has almost forgotten. There is a force *down* into the water before there is a thrust up. There is a famous Byzantine mosaic in Ravenna in which Neptune is sitting under the water beside Jesus. The water is depth, and it is penitential because in John's apocalyptic message the baptism in the water was for the "remission of sins" before the cataclysmic day of judgment. What happened to these apocalyptic elements and to Jesus himself by the interiorization of them is a study in itself. Research into this is now being conducted. Also in the baptism, the spirit as a dove (the bird of Venus and Astarte, and of Noah's covenant) describes symbolically the movement of what is happening. The beloved son, including the eros quality and the words "This day have I begotten thee," (alternate to the more familiar words) express the feminine principle clearly. Love and forgiveness and mercy are all there as partly opposed to and quite different from the message of John. Also the symbol of the wilderness to which Jesus moves immediately after the baptism, is that of the uncharted, the *massa confusa* of the alchemists - the chaos where one must find direction within.

A feminine symbol in the Gospels, appearing several times, is that of the cup as the container of life, of pain and suffering. The times Jesus holds it and relates to it are moments when eternity is held in the finite, in the intersection of the two worlds, and Jesus drinks and partakes or does not so that both he and the Divine are changed. The cup may be seen by each of us as the limited portion of the Infinite which is ours to deal with. The symbol of bread occurs over and over again in the parables. It is seen in its greatest mystery at the last supper where, with the wine, it becomes another great carrier of transformation.

In the Garden of Gethsemane (Mk. 14:32) there are three feminine aspects: first, the garden itself as an enclosure or *temenos*, a garden which I call the incubation of desire. (A garden which is significant to contrast to the Garden of Eden.) Second, there is Jesus' prayer in Gethsemane. The mysticism of Jesus is the mysticism of relatedness versus absorption or identification in Buber's distinction. Jesus does not say "Thy will be done." He does not say "My will." He says, "Not my will but Thine." He works in the framework of existential relatedness. And thirdly, the feminine is seen in the regressive symbol of the disciples sleeping at this crucial moment. (It is illuminating to compare this scene to the storm at sea, to the parable on importunity, and to other feminine "regressive" symbols.)

We move then to the last great moment of his life experience, that of the cross and the crucifixion itself, both historically and mythologically. Here is the movement of fulfillment of the utmost devotion of Jesus and the utmost manifestation of the purposes of God. Where do we find the feminine symbols here? There is the vertical thrust, that which reaches up into the infinite and down into the earth. (Compare it to the Jewish mystical translation of Psalm 130 which has the reading, not "out of the depths I cry unto Thee," but "I cry unto Thee who art in the depths.") This down thrust of the vertical dimension is one which has often been forgotten. In this sense the vertical brings together the opposites of masculine — up and feminine — down. And the horizontal finite dimension includes the relation to the human, symbolically portrayed as the thieves on either side of Jesus. Their presence as representatives of dark, imperfect, struggling mankind, help us feel in addition to the vertical thrust, the opposites which Jesus took upon himself on the way to fulfillment.

The women at earth roots of the cross also bring in the feminine quality and become the important presences in the next step after the crucifixion.

And central beyond all these elements is the man himself with his wounds — Jesus — Jesus as Son of man, representing the total loyalty to the Totality.

However we interpret the events after the crucifixion, something happened that shook the Mediterranean world, and started the new religion of Christianity. Historically this was the moment of "death" before the rebirth of the spirit in the disciples, and all that issued from it. It may be compared mythologically to the descent and the night sea journey in the solar ship of the Egyptians. At the tomb one has the presence of the women. The masculine has fled. The women are there for the carrying and the caring, the next step. They are the tenders of birth and death, the nurturing principle, those who take care of the human situation, alert, responsive, concerned as perhaps they must always be when there are human crises. They carry the grief and the suffering at a personal, physical, psychic, and spiritual level. The presence of the feminine assures that the spirit which cannot die will be reborn. (It has been impressive at various times in the last eight or nine years to observe the wives of the assassinated leaders in our country, and to see how they, too, were carriers of grief and vessels of pain, bearing the feminine principle with tremendous dignity and discipline).

Because Jesus' tomb is cared for, it can become "the manger" where the new birth begins in the disciples. Out of the historical developing experience of the disciples, 300 years later pagan archetypal mystery symbols were inevitably included in projected forms. The idea of the birth of the son inwardly, out of the feminine principle becomes the Christmas nativity story. The virginal, pure vessel is the inner womb which, impregnated, gives birth to the divine child or self which is in each one of us. We have forgotten this, making it outer. To return to the beginning, the forgotten feminine in the forgotten Gospels may be a deep resource for helping us to actualize and incarnate within ourselves our almost forgotten child, whose birth in our souls is the essence of our longing to fulfill ourselves in evolution, and in the creative process which we call God.

SYMBOLISM IN THE BIBLE

The most central observation that can be made today from the insights of all schools of depth psychology is the fact that modern man is lacking a relationship to himself, and his own total personality, and that there are large areas within his psyche which are unknown, unconscious, lying dormant, which need to be used, to be redeemed, to be brought into consciousness, both for their sake and for his sake. To my mind, it has been especially the contribution of the Analytical Psychology of Dr. Jung that helps us to understand this unconscious area as containing creative potentials, positive as well as negative, universal images (archetypes) which bear much energy and which are fundamental in predisposing us toward certain ways of acting and behaving. This area of the unconscious, personal as well as collective, is, for Jung, expressed primarily through the symbol – which always refers to something beyond itself that is essentially unknown and unassimilated. A symbol reflects something mysterious to which it refers, something with ever-expanding meanings.

The special dilemma of the Protestant lies in the fact that he is cut off from his unconscious reservoir in himself, that he is split, in his consciously-held ideas or in his theological concepts, from his own inner realities and is unaware of what lies under the surface keeping him in a divided and sick state. One sees this sickness in analytic situations where dreams point up what is really going on inside, what needs yet to be assimilated. The Protestant is divorced, for historical reasons which I have previously stated, from his own deeper levels. Or, to say it another way, he is confronted by a great dearth of symbolic imagery in his whole religious setting.

Is this lack of imagery and symbolism because he is cut off? Or is he cut off because of the lack of being related to ritual and symbolic expression? Historically separation from these was certainly the price paid for the Protestant thrust of individuality out of the Catholic structure. At that time symbolism was belittled and became almost defunct, and now its absence affects the psyche and slowly damages it more and more. The Protestant needs the inner symbolic expression for the fulfillment of himself and his own history.

After some discussion on the Protestant dilemma, I was asked by someone if it were my implication that it is better to be a Catholic than to be a Protestant, because I had seemed to imply that the Catholic had not lost contact with the symbol in the same way. I want to make it clear that of course I am making no such judgment. I believe deeply that each one of us has to find his or her own destiny and answer to the question of fulfillment in life in terms of his own roots, his own background. Dr. Jung has pointed out that if any patient is better off in a church than not in one, then he belongs in the church. The Catholic has the advantage of his unconscious psyche being contained in the symbolism of the church, but he does not thereby automatically have a conscious relationship to it. It may even be that he does not have as much opportunity for individual development, but I do not pretend to pass judgment on whether one is better than another; they are simply structurally and psychically different. Each of us must find his own way. As a Jungian analyst, I am naturally concerned to investigate this problem primarily with Protestants but also with Jewish people and increasingly with people with Catholic backgrounds.

By way of example of what I mean by experiencing the symbol, I would like to tell of two experiences I have had that had to do with observation of what it means to be rooted in the symbolic life and to express it, and what seems to be its healing and therapeutic power.

A few years ago I had the opportunity of vacationing two weeks near Santa Fe, New Mexico, during Holy Week. On Good Friday, I was in the small town of Truchas to observe the procession of the Penitentes. The Penitentes, as probably you know, are a small sect within the Catholic Church, rather frowned on by the church but, I understand, have very recently more or less been brought back into the fold. I presume the reason for the church's question about them lay in their very literal interpretation of the Christian drama and the Christian myth. Until very recent years they actually went through a crucifixion on Good Friday, with a voluntary sacrifice on the part of a living man. That, I am told, has been changed, although they still do practice flagellation. Of course there was no opportunity for an outsider to observe their most secret rites which occur the Thursday night before Good Friday in the *morada*, their secret meeting place. But on the morning of Good Friday they leave the *morada*, and move in a procession through the town to the church, arriving there at noon for the three hours of watch. As I stood in this very beautiful setting, in this little town in the high New Mexico plateau, I was surprisingly moved, as this small procession of people came slowly down the road towards the church. The men carried effigies of the Christ figure, and behind them came the old women of the community, very old women with dramatically lined faces, carrying effigies of the Mother. There was a minor lamenting sort of chant, and a periodic stop for prayers, with everyone kneeling down in the dust. I admit I felt that I was in the presence of a great Pieta. I would not pretend to know what this ritual meant to the people in the procession. I can only say that here was a symbolic ritual – the Christian myth being literally portrayed and lived by these people. That it carried something for them I would have no question.

Two days later, there was the opportunity to go to some of the Indian pueblos to observe the Indian corn dances, spring festivals to the corn goddess before the planting of the crops. Here, by contrast, (and yet not so much by contrast), was another ritual relation to the symbol. We stood in the plaza, the great open space in the middle of the pueblo, observing the women who were not in the dance sitting against their adobe houses and on their roofs, wearing their bright-colored blankets and scarves. Suddenly out of the two kivas (their secret ceremonial meeting-place) came literally hundreds of dancers. One dance was primarily for children, and on later days it included children, men and women, merging and dancing in the way which D. H. Lawrence so graphically described in *Mornings in Mexico*. There was the chanting to the drumbeat, the prayers, the songs whose content of course we did not know. We could only imagine and feel into it as the dancers came to the middle of the plaza and then danced for hours on end. It was my first experience of Indian ritual, and somewhere it hit very much in the middle of my solar plexus. One woman (an Anglo, as the Indians call us) asked one of the Indian women, "Don't the children get tired dancing?" The very simple answer by the Indian was, "But this is the way they learn." I could not help but reflect what it would mean for a child to be brought up with the sense of communal relationship and of deep ritual which this kind of situation affords. I spoke with an Indian woman who was brought up in the pueblo which we were visiting (a university-educated Indian who now lives in Santa Fe with her husband, both of them Catholic). I asked about the inner and outer problems of trying to bring together the two cultures of the Indian and Catholic, of the pueblo and of the city. She made this comment: "I try to tell the people in the church that when we are singing and dancing to the earth goddess, we are also celebrating Christ and Mary, but it's very hard for some of the people in the church to understand."

The Penitentes, and the Indians in their dance from the kiva, for hours on end singing to the powers that they revere – the corn goddess, the earth goddess, the fertility symbol in the whole universe – here are experiences of people who are rooted in their own tradition, experiences for which it is very hard to find parallels in our Protestantism. How can we begin to get back into the symbolism inherent in our own religious culture?

One of the ways, and the way which I want to speak of today, is through an understanding of, a responding to, and opening of one's self to the symbols and the mythic motifs which are found in the Bible, which is, after all, the record in the Judaic-Christian tradition of man's search for consciousness. To see the Bible as containing a wealth of *symbolic* material which could be for us psychologically healing and therapeutic is difficult because of our very familiarity with it. We think we know all about what "Bible stories" mean, for most unfortunately we heard them talked about in Sunday school, on the whole in a very dull and boring way. Also the modern religious liberal has tended to "throw the baby out with the bath" and when he found that the Bible wasn't "true" in the sense of literal, historical reality he thought it did not have any meaning. I am not concerned here with the distinction between those parts of the Bible which have an historical basis and those which do not. This is the scholar's task. At the moment I want to treat all Biblical material as one would treat any myth, legend or fairy tale, as being symbolic expressions of the realities and archetypes within us. I want to speak of what it would mean to be open to them, to be moved by the numinous quality of them, whether we are Jewish or whether we are Christian.

The stories in the Old Testament, the parables of Jesus in the New Testament, as well as many other parts, such as Psalms, are full of rich, imaginative pictures which are symbolic of some spiritual and psychological truth. The Bible is replete with the classic symbols of mankind, and with mythic motifs which are symbolic of the aspects of the process of growth and of development. These symbols and motifs appear in the Old Testament, beginning in Genesis with the great creation stories which are comparable to other great creation myths—in this case, certainly very close to and influenced by the Babylonian - Sumerian tradition. There is the story of the flood. Later, in the Old Testament come symbolic expressions in the visions of the prophets, such as Isaiah, Ezekiel, and Daniel, with such symbols as water, flood, fire, mountain, the beast, Satan as central psychological reality. The sacrificial lamb – found, certainly, in other pagan rites – is seen in the story of Abraham and Isaac and is later identified with the figure of Jesus. In the New Testament are the cross with its attendant symbols of the two thieves, the women at the foot of the cross, the veil of the temple being rent, the soldiers, the cross itself as one expression of the *mandala* form (defined by Jung as "that four-foldness which is the framework, or which expresses the framework or the dimension of the Self"). These are only a few of the many immense symbols which one finds throughout the Bible.

There are also what Jung and Kerenyi have called the "mythologems", the mythic motifs related to the journey to find the Self, the journey to individuation. These motifs include the journey itself, the crossing of the water, the night-sea journey, the motif of disobedience, the hiding of the newborn infant (such as one finds in the story of Moses and the story at the beginning of the Christian myth), the motif of the sacrifice, and others.

Out of this wealth of possible material I would like to take two stories from the Old Testament, and then two or three references from the New Testament which I think may give us a clue as to how we could begin to read and to feel into this Biblical material. Let me first of all take a story certainly very well known to most of you, the story of Jacob and Esau (Genesis, Chapter 27) and Jacob's stealing of the blessing. You remember the story. The father, Isaac, is about to die and he tells Esau, the older son, to go get savory food. He says, "Go and get it that I may eat and bless you before the Lord before I die." Rebekah, the wife, overhears this and intervenes by going to the younger son, Jacob, and telling Jacob to dress like Esau and to go and deceive his father and to receive the blessing. Jacob protests, but Rebekah says "Upon me be your curse; only obey me." Rebekah helps Jacob in the deception of putting on the clothes and acting in such a way that his father will be deceived, and Jacob does carry off the act. He gets the blessing, as earlier he had gotten the birthright.

What does this mean? Whether one takes it at a mythological level or at a very individual level—that is, as applying just to the development of one person—it seems to say that the younger brother, or the younger part, the lesser part, in some ways the inferior part, has to deceive, has to do the illegitimate thing in order to get blessed. This represents a profound psychological truth. It is the same idea, or signifies the same thing, as in the classic story of the Garden of Eden where Eve has to disobey the command of Yahweh in order to become conscious, in order to be related to Adam, in order to know the difference between good and evil, in order to be related to life itself. In the story of the Prodigal Son, although it is not concerned directly with the theme of disobedience, the Prodigal Son has in one sense to disobey the father by taking his inheritance and leaving all the old values to find new values. He has to go away and go through a difficult period and return at a very new level of development, which his father then speaks of as a rebirth. In a certain way, the story of Mary and Martha in the New Testament represents the same theme. Mary gets a blessing by going against all the ordinary collective patterns, which considerably annoys her sister Martha. Mary does not do the expected thing. Rather, she does the different thing, and yet she seems to be the one who receives richness in return. In all these stories there is a daring to be an individual by going against the usual and collective ways. There has been a thrust forward and a thrust out of the containing patterns. There are many other parallels. The same theme occurs in the Greek myths of Prometheus stealing the fire, of Amor and Psyche, and of Pandora's box. There is a taboo which has to be broken in order for consciousness to be achieved. The forbidden somehow becomes the saving element.

Whether at a personal or at a cosmological level, there evidently has to be disobedience to a partial in order to be whole. We have to do the forbidden, that which is condemned by the "status quo", to redeem what has been lost. We have to integrate what has become dark, repressed, rejected, in order to go on to integration. A taboo, a collective pattern, even the command of the gods, has to be broken; and most mysteriously and most paradoxically, the gods seem to be behind both the taboo and the thrust out of the taboo into the new pattern.

Another classic motif in the Old Testament is found in the later story (Genesis 32) of Jacob's struggle with the angel. Again, you will remember the story. By a river-bank, before daybreak, Jacob wrestles with a male figure who is usually referred to as an angel. The angel puts the thigh of Jacob out of joint, because Jacob will not let him go. Jacob replies, "I will not let you go until you bless me." The angel then changes the name Jacob to Israel, and he says, "For you have striven with God and with men and have prevailed." Jacob later replies, "I have seen God face to face, and yet my life is preserved." The symbols here have great significance at the level of mythological development, and also for us personally. Here is symbolized a deep encounter and the courage to stay with a problem until an answer is found.

At an every-day level we see over and over the need to stay with a difficulty instead of to flee or to evade a problem. This struggle happens by the river-bank, on that threshold between the conscious and the unconscious. It happens at daybreak —daybreak being, as it is in nature, the moment of the coming of light or the dawning of a new stage in consciousness. This is the courage which most of us lack, and because we lack it we cannot say that we live a life in which we feel blessed, which we so need to feel. Out of this encounter there emerges the crippled hero, crippled as Jacob then is, because in any encounter with the powers that are beyond our conscious psyche and beyond our own personal unconscious, and perhaps beyond us even more transcendently (the suprapersonal powers) we have to be willing to suffer. We have to be willing to receive scars as the price for expanded consciousness and self-fulfillment. In fact, there is no fulfillment and no consciousness unless we are willing to carry the burden of having, in whatever form it comes, the "wounded thigh".

Turning from the Old Testament to the New Testament, let me first take a scene which certainly has an historical basis, but which represents, archetypally and symbolically, I think, another aspect of the encounter such as we saw with Jacob and the angel. It is a scene very rich in symbolism. It is the scene of the baptism of Jesus at the hands of John, and Jesus' subsequent struggle in the wilderness with Satan. To remind you of the elements of the story: Jesus comes to be baptized by John. He descends into the water in order to meet the demand of John's movement, which is that of repentance. His descent into the river is for a purpose; it is not meaningless. As he emerges from the water, the heavens are "rent asunder", "the Spirit as a dove" descends, and a voice speaks, calling him "beloved Son". Immediately thereafter Jesus withdraws to the wilderness where he struggles with the figure of Satan in the so-called three great "temptations", where he is ministered to by the "wild beasts" and "angels", and out of which he emerges with new conviction and direction.

What does the scene of the baptism represent that could have meaning to us? It represents an experience of submersion and submission to the flowing unconscious, and an emergence from it with a totally new sense of relationship to that which Jesus called Father, and a new sense of direction. In the wilderness experience, Jesus meets whatever is the reality of Satan's proposals, confronts this reality, struggles with it, refuses it, and emerges into life and a new vocation. Although very different, because of a very much higher and different level of development, from the story of Jacob's encounter with the angel there are some elements in common. Let us look for a minute at the symbols. In the first place, there is the descent into the water. The water as the vast feminine container is a classic symbol of the fluid, moving element within ourselves. The spirit is ordinarily thought of as masculine, but here I would say it is personified in a feminine way by the dove, the bird of Venus and of Aphrodite, which may suggest the more feminine qualities of gentleness and softness. Certainly at the time of the New Testament the spirit was not thought of primarily as feminine, as it begins to be in the baptism scene. Then there is the experience of Jesus feeling himself not only as a son, whatever that meant, but as "beloved Son". The word "beloved", I would think, also contains a feminine quality, the quality of Eros, relationship, love. The voice speaking is a classic symbol in myth and legend as well as in the dreams of modern man. It seems to symbolize inner wisdom and the articulation of wisdom, something which comes from the eternal, the more universal, the deeper archetypal stream and intrudes into time, moving into the consciousness of a man. Also there is the symbol of the wilderness itself, representing the uncharted, the unknown areas of ourselves. There is not space here to speak of

Satan and what happens in the development of that complex concept which goes back through the whole Old Testament.

It is interesting to think briefly of the relationship of the baptism experience to the story of Jacob struggling with the angel. Two points of similarity strike me. In both cases I am reminded of a line of poetry of W. H. Auden, "The distresses of choice are our chance to be blessed." If we could take that statement in relation to the two stories we could get a rich revelation as to what the choice was which Jacob and Jesus had to make which led to the experience of being blessed. Another point of similarity is the fact that both were made to suffer. I said earlier that the achievement of consciousness at a human level always involves some kind of pain. Jacob was left with a wounded thigh. Jesus received his wounds in what he had to face in the crucifixion.

Let us look finally at a few of the fundamental symbols found in some of the parables which are used in the teachings of Jesus in the New Testament. It was part of the genius of Jesus that he used images so basic and earthly and relevant at that time, and they are certainly relevant to us today. For instance, what is he speaking of when he says that the thing for which it is worth selling everything that one has is the pearl of great price? Why does he take a pearl as the ultimate value? The pearl comes from the oyster in the sea. The pearl is a natural jewel, a living jewel, built around an irritation of living matter. One can imagine the surprise of man when he first came upon this beautiful object in the center of a mass of shelled life. Symbolically, not only is the pearl the divine inner element, the valuable jewel we all want to find, of great beauty and rarity, but it is to be found in most unexpected and unappealing places, and is produced by irritation. What a wealth of psychological material there is in this for our careful consideration!

What is Jesus speaking of in the parable of the man building the house on sand, which fell when the storms came, and the man who built his house on rock so that it stood when the storms came? The rock is an age-old symbol of primal material with the quality of permanence and eternality. That there is something like that in ourselves is a reassuring picture, in marked contrast with the shifting nature of sand which we know too well. Not long ago, a patient of mine had a dream in which she was sitting in a room with her feet in sand. She had lost her shoes, and the sand was moving up, covering her feet, and beginning to cover her legs. The sand was falling from the walls of the house. She knew how important it was for her to get up immediately and to leave the room before the sand overcame her. That seems to me to be a contemporary expression of the symbol of sand on which many of us have tried to build our inner houses. This parable of the building of the two different houses stresses implicitly the structuring of life. It stresses the fact of the activity of the work which man must do. In contrast, what is Jesus speaking of when he says in another parable that the seed that a man casts upon the earth grows of itself? The seed is planted by man; the man goes to sleep; then the blade, then the ear, then the full grain in the ear appears. Is he not, through pointing out the nature of growth in the natural world, describing the nature of growth in the inner world? For this parable, too, is about the "kingdom of God", or, to put it in modern terms, about the discovery of the potentiality of our own inner selves. The age-old fertility symbol of grain, used in so many of the mysteries, is a symbol of the miraculousness of growth. If the parable of the house stresses the work of building that the conscious, or the ego, side of man must do, this parable of the grain stresses that even though man goes to sleep, and perhaps must, for a period of what might be thought of as incubation (once he is started and the seed has been planted), there is something that proceeds without his help, and this is the activity from "the other side".

Teilhard de Chardin, Jesuit, scientist, paleontologist, talked effectively about the evolutionary character of Process – with his concept that "Omega" – spirit in substance – grows from matter, *materia*, towards and into the "noosphere", which includes past, present, and future, personal and situational.

These, then, are but a few examples of the symbols and mythic motifs which are to be found in the Bible. I hope that perhaps it has become clear that the value for the Protestant who wants to fulfill himself, who wants to find his lost meaning, who wants to delve into the unconscious for the purpose of becoming more conscious, is that he may return to this wealth of material as containing symbolic vitality. If he will relate to it, if he will feel and think into this material, his unconscious being may be much enlivened and enriched. From this he may find symbols in his culture which are also expressive of his totality. Thus he may find help in the living out of his own personal myth. It is possible.

THE PROTESTANT DILEMMA

Between the Protestant and the realization of his own soul lies, paradoxically, what I call the "Protestant dilemma". Four dreams of four contemporary men and women illustrate certain aspects of this dilemma. The histories of these people are not important for our purposes. Some were members of a church and some not. I am concerned only with these expressions which came unbidden from the unconscious depths to the complete surprise of the dreamers, and which express the core of the dilemma. The dreams are as follows:

1. I am going down a stair-case into the earth through a dark tunnel. In center of opening, surrounded by radiant light, was a Christ-like figure which was so startling I fell to my knees.

2. I return to the church of my childhood, stand in the middle of the church, and the minister then baptizes me all over with wine. I am deeply moved, and know in the dream that it involved transformation for me.

3. I am in hell and a very Satanic looking figure is trying to capture me. I call and call for someone to come and help me and release me. Flames are there too.

4. I am carrying in my arms a new baby dressed in black and white. I'm aware that its life and mine depend on my care of it. The baby's name was Judah, and in the dream I realized this symbolized the Kingdom of Judah which was to be the land in the Old Testament from which the Christ was to be born. I was surprised because I had given no thought to Judaism as fundamental in Christianity.

These various symbols, Christ, baptism, wine, Satan and Judah, can all be recognized as central in the Christian faith. I am not concerned with their meaning or interpretation here. The important common element is that they appear unbidden, un-understood, in rational people whose religious faith did not include such symbols, and yet in each case the person was moved by them. There was a numinous, dynamic quality in the appearance of these rejected or unknown symbols which, on being understood, had healing and therapeutic value for the dreamers. In each case the dream, when taken seriously as an expression in symbolic form of the central life-affirming energies within, altered the patient's state, but not until the person had gone through the shock of knowing these elements were different and absolutely "other" from his conscious attitude or belief.

How and why do these dream symbols define the Protestant dilemma? Insofar as most Protestants do not know the contents and realities of their inmost soul, have no living connection with them, and are thus cut off from the true roots of spiritual and religious vitality, the appearance of such symbols points up the dilemma. Such dreams suggest a definite split between the conscious and unconscious beliefs. Moreover, they suggest that there are living and dynamic forces in the unconscious which are expressed in traditional symbols regardless of consciously-held ideas or theological concepts. These kinds of dreams could be duplicated over and over again by people (whether inside or outside the church) who would consciously refuse or give no assent to the idea represented in the symbol. Failing to find meaning and being symptom-ridden, such people turn to depth-psychology, usually quite unaware that behind many of their symptoms is just this religious ferment in their psyche which is driving them to search for an answer.

Let me discuss this dilemma briefly, look at its historical roots, attempt to evaluate it in its positive and negative aspects, and finally consider how a psychological study of the Gospels may offer some creative solution. The first aspect of the dilemma is that Protestantism at its inception broke loose from the authoritarianism of the dominant church, from what seemed bondage to the dogma and creed which had, to these pioneers, become only intellectual statements. It found freedom to refute the idea of the Trinity, or to disbelieve the Virgin Birth as physical fact, or to question the incarnation of God in man as Christ. Protestants could either do away with or alter all ritual and sacrament (as with the Quakers) or water communion down from wine to grape-juice.

The Protestant could, in his new-found and exciting individual freedom, "explain" things and thus do away with them without necessarily assimilating the content of the thing which he was explaining away. This development of the recognition of the right of the individual to exert free choice and decision, as opposed to the authoritarianism of the church and the Bible, went with the new emphasis on the rational side of man and the growth of the scientific spirit. It is Dr. Jung's thought which today is psychologically helping us see the implication of this revolution when these dogmas, creeds, and sacraments were "explained away". Actually they do remain as psychic realities within because they are representatives of archetypal motifs with which we must come to terms if we are in the Judaic-Christian tradition. Beneath the level of the personal unconscious is what Dr. Jung calls the collective unconscious, or the archetypal level. These archetypes, very simply, are universal and non-personal images which contain energy and predispose us to act or behave in certain ways, as for example the Great Mother, the old Wise Man, the Divine Child, the Self, the Journey. They are gripping and determinative.

The doctrines of the Trinity and of the Virgin Birth, and the institution of the Mass, are excellent examples of where archetypes are raised to the conscious level and transmitted into ritual. We may disbelieve the dogma, reject the sacraments, yet somehow they often contain vitality and truth. If, as has been said by one theologian, the "Trinity is a revelation not only of God but of man", if behind the Virgin birth story we have the primordial image of the continual emergence of the Divine Child in the psyche, if in the Mass we have a Christian expression of pre-Christian social rituals, then it must be with the greatest caution that we throw them out! If they are only ideas we can reject them, but if they are dogmas and rituals which express and re-enact archetypal motifs, then we must know what we are doing.

Whereas the first aspect of this Protestant dilemma is separation from the moving irrational qualities of the symbols contained in the dogma, the second aspect of the dilemma centers on the emphasis of the rational and "good" side of man, and therefore on a certain disbelief in the devils. When the confessional and the need for absolution by the church were eliminated by Protestantism, the greatest safety-valve for the "devil's power" was eliminated. As long as one could confess one's sins, it was easier to admit them. But this new step of rejection of the means whereby sin was dealt with altered the situation, and it became a more difficult personal matter.

Recently a liberal minister, speaking of his beliefs, said somewhat hesitantly, "I believe in sin." My own reaction was, "Ye gods, he'd better!" How can we not believe in it when we see it all around us and within ourselves? The analysts' offices are filled with people with a sense of sin or guilt as symptomatic of revolt against the orthodox standards and ethical judgments, usually of their parents, but with little sense of the true objective meaning of sin, of themselves as sinners, as people who have not worked for wholeness, people who have failed their own potential, or, in Biblical terms, have not fulfilled their end of the covenant of relatedness of man and God, or man and the supra-personal power. The fact remains that the Protestant has not come to terms enough with the reality of the devil as a psychic entity in his own soul. This cuts him off from part of himself, as does the resulting dearth of imagery and symbol, because his chance for redemption and fundamental change is based on the acknowledgement of his own split and divided heart and soul. And if we don't face this devil within we project him everywhere—which wrecks most organizations and relationships. Evil will not be eliminated or forgotten! If it is not met consciously it has its own way with us personally and impersonally. The shadow has to become a recognizable member of our own household, which requires great humility from us. Absolutely nothing is harder to face!

These then are the two parts of the dilemma: the separation of the conscious from the irrational and unconscious images, and the difficulty of taking individual responsibility for the devil. Where lie the historical roots of this? Whatever one's intellectual or theological beliefs, one must consider the formation of the church two thousand years ago as the expression of a new, vital, and living experience. What that experience was or how it came about, or even the relation of Jesus' teachings to it, is not my concern here. Something had happened; some new birth had occurred – a whole new conjunction had come about. Whether one said God had become man, Christ was born, the *logos* had been incarnated, all the arguments of the early church on the nature of God and the Christ and the logos were attempts to find a framework for some central, numinous event. But as so often happens, these experiences lost their power, and crystalized into creed and dogma.

At the outset, within the church the genuine aspects of symbol and ritual grew and, in fact, carried the original meaning of those symbols which were taken over from pagan and mystery religions. The mother goddess became the Virgin, the initiation rites of the early mysteries became part of the Christian baptismal ceremony, the cross as universal mandala became infused with new meaning. The Catholic church was and still is, to quote one theologian, "the great objectification of the unconscious of man". All the living realities in man's own soul are outside, and man can get in touch with them and participate to some extent in their meaning, although that participation may or may not be very conscious.

The Catholic church, too, provided a containment for the problem of the devil through the confessional, and retained authority for the individual. It defined the nature both of revelation and of individual action. The whole movement of the Renaissance, with its emphasis on the individual, stirred the souls of many within the church, and Dr. Jung has emphasized that such mystics as Meister Eckhart, Angelus Silesius, and Jacob Boehme, while retaining much of the symbolism of the church, opened up the possibility of a direct access to God through individual experience. These men were the forerunners for a Luther and a Zwingli who could assert and define the values of the Reformation and could carry further this possibility of an inner experience without the church's mediation, although sometimes too harshly.

Now may I return to a tentative evaluation of the positive and negative aspects of Protestantism? A review of these pluses and minuses is essential for any full consideration of the Protestant dilemma and its challenge. Four basic features seem to me to characterize Protestantism. Each of these may be weighed in its positive and negative aspect, and the challenges with which these present us may be examined.

First was the break with the authority of the Roman church and Pope, with the radical possibility that an individual could decide things for himself and act on his own conscience. The implication of this was that divine revelation was no longer accepted as having happened once and for all, complete in a moment of history. Now an individual could have his own unique intensive experience as valid, could have his own relationship to supra-personal forces. (This is psychologically treated in Jung's concept of the universal nature of the archetypes or collective images.) On the positive side, this break meant a tremendous new emphasis on the dignity and value of the individual. He was free in a new way and could be the bearer of his own decisions and the recipient of real revelation. But on the negative side this break led inevitably to a false definition of freedom, to a corruption of freedom evidenced in the confusion between freedom and license. The possibility of creative individuality often narrows into pseudo-individuality or individualism. That is, psychologically we have developed a formidable ego-centricity in place of a creative "I" which can act in relation to life and serve life because it comes from a deeper center. The new individual possibility has been misused, yet it is still potentially there to be used creatively. (The striking novel *The Nun's Story* seems to me a beautiful example of the Catholic-Protestant difference. The fact that at the end the nun must obey her own conscience rather than be obedient states the Protestant case. Yet it also has been interesting for me to see, as an analyst, how many Protestants reading the book respond favorably to the Catholic position of obedience in its positive aspect, just because as Protestants they have gone so far in negative freedom that they long for something comparable to Catholic discipline.)

The second feature of Protestantism has been the emphasis on the rational side, the thinking mental side, with the subsequent rejection or reduction of dogmas and creeds and symbolic contents. Protestantism saw man as having a rational and clear mind with the possibility of using that mind critically and analytically. This was a great step forward, although hard for us to evaluate today because we have swung so far to that rational side that we are in desperate need of coming back to a balance. In fact this constitutes the negative side of this second feature. This rational emphasis led to a cut-offness from the inner world of the symbol. It thus becomes conspicuous (as many observers have noted) that the outstanding characteristic of most modern Protestant churches is a dearth of imagery. The spiritual and psychological importance of this is that it cuts us off from the living flow of the unconscious where the religious images are born and where the dynamic roots for any alive religion are to be found. Dr. Jung has said, "Protestantism forfeits the salvation that is given to those who know the living symbol." Yet we long for the living symbol. For example, many of us just "live through" Christmas (which is the impression most Americans give!) Sometimes we "experience" it. So often during the Christmas season I pause to think of the millions of Americans lustily singing Christmas carols, and I venture to say that they have not the remotest idea what is in the words and their meanings, and yet during that time something is different within them; something is touched. Through this repression of symbols from the vital archetypal stream comes the loss of that most central God-man image which Jung calls the Self. With this loss one of the fateful and fatal problems of Protestantism develops. God becomes an idea, a mental product, or an intuition, and not a reality in the soul. Putting it otherwise, the Protestant loses his fear of God and sees God only as something to be loved, admired or worshipped. In the words of Rudolph Otto, those qualities of awe and reverence which inevitably are present if God is a "living thing" disappear. We fail to grasp the numinous and mysterious, or to let ourselves be grasped by it. Also in our denial of this side, we lose contact with the Christ-image in our unconscious, which is inevitably there because of our background.

A third feature affecting Protestantism and increasing the dilemma has been the development of the whole scientific field. Because we know this is probably the West's greatest achievement, we need spend the least time on it. And perhaps the negative side of it is all too apparent to us. The most pertinent comment on it, I think, is Dr. Robert Oppenheimer's comment at an American Psychological Association convention that we have lost the sense of the miraculous, and we must keep open to it. This scientific emphasis has penetrated most areas of scholarship, including scientific research into the Bible. No longer under Protestantism was the Bible a sacrosanct divine thing which could not be touched by ordinary human research. It is hard for us at this later period to realize how radical that was, and what the development of the field of historical literary criticism has really meant. But a very negative side of this has been the split between history and myth, and the subsequent repression of consideration of myth in the Bible until very recently. In the New Testament, a study of the Jesus of history has made many liberals suspicious of any value being attached to mythological or non-historical portions. The Virgin Birth dogma has been rejected as historical fact, therefore it is considered as meaningless and not to be thought about. Again it is the emphasis of Analytical Psychology primarily that is pushing us to revise these notions and to ask from where do these stories or motifs come that appear in all religions. What psychological truth do they hold for us if they are not historically true and factual?

The final feature of Protestantism to be considered

here has to do with the status of the devil, or the problem of sin. On the positive side, the Catholic idea of confession-absolution led to the possibility of an individual relationship to, and facing of, the dark side of being. This was a marked development in the achievement of consciousness. It meant that something was now available for personal reckoning. But just because the problem of sin was so appalling, Satan practically had to be damned! Christianity has denied him through projection, rationalized him, or tried to assume he is all a fake. Before looking at the challenge which this problem of evil poses, let us examine the answer which many people today are finding in the neo-orthodox point of view, taken in its most general and broad meaning.

In 1936, I attended a seminar in the form of a panel discussion between Henry Nelson Weiman, Gregory Vlastos, Reinhold Neibuhr and Paul Tillich. Most of you will know something of some of these men and their positions. At the conscious rational level, my sympathies were entirely with Weiman and Vlastos. What they had to say articulated my own embryonic viewpoint. But the messages which stirred me and stayed with me were those of Neibuhr and Tillich. Although I disagreed then, and still would disagree, with much of their theology, I recognize that they included elements lacking in the essence of liberal Protestantism as I have been discussing it. What are these elements? First, there is an admission of human nature, and its "unhealth" and guilt and consequent need and possibility for redemption, that seems emotionally gripping and stirring. And I now recognize that there was a *tremendum* and depth in the way Niebuhr and Tillich talked of the reality of God that was different from the others. Secondly, what these men meant by "Christ" obviously referred to something different from Jesus and had to be taken into account, which I certainly wasn't doing at that time. I do not feel their way is necessarily the answer, but if it is provocative it more than ever can send us back to consider the challenges of our present dilemma.

What does emerge from this evaluation for any of us as individuals? Four challenging possibilities seem apparent.

To begin with, the next step in religious consciousness must include the balance of the opposites of the rational and irrational. I have stressed how one-sidedly rational we have become. The irrational, it seems, either appears primarily negatively in explosions like war or positively in the arts, or it is held in prison in the unconscious or is projected. We need to work at the level of our personal life for a new synthesis of the irrational with our rational and developed side.

Intimately bound up with the preceding is the need for expression of those deep, creative levels within which is contained the healing power. We need new symbols, or a fresh interpretation of old symbols. I mean by a "new symbol" not a completely original entity, but rather a new use of or response to a symbol in ways not previously experienced. Old symbols already time-honored and valid, may be revivified if our attitude toward them is changed. Then they move us. It is not unimportant that many Protestants will go to an Episcopal or Roman Catholic Church for something in them. For example, the person kneeling in prayer before a Virgin Mary statue is letting the divine Mother element be activated within as a healing force.

Thirdly, we Protestants are challenged with the real problem of facing our inner shadow and dealing with it. Because it is so great a burden, it is easier to deny it, to rationalize it, or to protect it. (In this connection, the statement by Jesus about the beams and the motes has not yet been improved upon!) We must take more seriously what Laurens van der Post in *Venture to the Interior* calls our divided selves, and honor the need to love the dark brother within, whom we certainly can not love if we do not know of his existence, or will not admit it. The terrible consequence is the hate of the dark brother in the world.

Dr. Jung has written, "The Protestant is left to God alone. For him there is no confession or absolution. He has to digest his sins himself . . . and because the absence of a suitable ritual has put it beyond his reach he is none too sure of God's grace. Hence the present alertness of the

Protestant conscience – which makes him uncomfortable. But because of this the Protestant has a unique chance to realize his sin to a degree that is beyond the reach of the Catholic who has confession. The Protestant is left to his tensions which go on sharpening his conscience — and a bad conscience can be a gift of heaven, a veritable grace if used in the interests of the higher self-criticism. And self-criticism is essential in every effort to understand one's own personality."

Perhaps the greatest possibility is that, due to the whole historical development, it is the Protestant who, if he will face these opposites, if he will take the inner journey, if he will accept his own dark side, has the unique chance of having a deep and genuine individual religious experience. In Analytical Psychology this experience is called individuation. Because the Protestant is finding that the symbols with which he has been content, and which have held and contained him, are breaking their hold on him, he can work towards a new creative center of Being. This work is the ultimate challenge, I believe. Can it be met? That it will involve suffering is almost self-evident, because no new way, as no birth, is without its labor pains. And we do not like to suffer.

To my mind, one of the ways for the Protestant to revitalize the symbols, and heal the split in his divided soul, is by a direct confrontation with the life and teaching of Jesus. Not Jesus the historical prophet, nor Jesus the dogmatic Christ — but something else which I shall try to define. This consideration of the material in the Synoptic Gospels is, to my mind, one of the most promising answers to our dilemma. Before I try to say why I think this is true, I need to say a word as to what such a study is *not* and what it *is*.

If one starts to study the Gospels of Matthew, Mark and Luke, on the assumption that Jesus was and still is to be identified with the Christ of dogma, two things must be noted. In the first place one is starting with a preconception and prejudice that keeps one from seeing what may actually be in the gospels. Secondly, this identification of Jesus with the Christ of dogma is not the conscious liberal Protestant position, and at a deeper symbolic level this has led to a confused image of the Christ figure as the carrier of the Self. What people think consciously, and what they feel, or have in the unconscious, are quite disparate.

On the other hand, merely to study the gospels in order to get at what we ordinarily call the historical Jesus or the prophet is not adequate. To study the Synoptic Gospels to get at this Jesus is in no sense new. The whole field of liberal theology has done this, has attempted to get Jesus out of creed and dogma and to see him as teacher, reformer, Rabbi, idealist. It has been the center of Protestant research for the past one hundred and fifty years. But this historical Jesus has been almost completely separated from the deeper levels of the unconscious, has been identified with the rational side, and therefore his message has been diluted. In a reaction against his being the symbol-carrier, the dogmatic Christ of orthodoxy, he has been pushed to the opposite pole.

What I feel to be the essence of the content of the Synoptic Gospels, if approached open-mindedly both from the standpoint of freedom from dogma (as far as possible) and from rational bias is this: Jesus is seen as a figure who himself achieved a deep sense of fulfillment, integration, consciousness through his relation to something beyond his conscious being — what he called God. He was remarkably lucid on how he achieved real Life, how other men may achieve it. He saw the object of devotion, God, as something within and without — although he experienced in a different language the dynamic essence of the Self, or the God-image within. He struggled with and knew the reality of Satan. His energy was deeply focussed on his own relation to the Christ-expectation of the day. How he solved it is crucial.

I could point up the essence of what I consider the core value of the Synoptic Gospels by raising a few questions. What was Jesus' own relation to the Christ image? Did he identify with it, or reject it? How does this go with the Christian doctrines that have identified him with it? What and who was Satan to Jesus? How did he see him and meet him? How do we integrate evil today? What does Jesus have to say about the relation of the precepts of Judaism and any new elements he brought? What about his relation to the sacraments of baptism and wine? Jesus included, I feel, the value of the Protestant position in his insistence on individual choice; he conveyed the deeply Jewish creative attitude toward God as far more moving and real than it is to most of us; and he suggested in many rich parables and analogies the archetypal level of symbol contained in the Roman Catholic church. And, if one is open to this material, one sees that Jesus asked over and over the one significant question: What are you doing about your own life? After a lecture I gave on the Gospels and Analytical Psychology, one person of considerable maturity (and with knowledge whereof he spoke) wrote this to me: "The Unitarians also grasped Jesus as a man. But they never saw him as the man living the deeper fate of greater consciousness towards the Self. Rather they stripped the whole experience of the dynamics of the inner and outer (the projected symbol) and presented us with a purer and more sterile ethic."

Surely this kind of approach to our Protestant dilemma is not the only answer—but I have no hesitancy in saying that because our religious heritage centers around Jesus (Christ) we must come to terms with him in some way. We must understand not only the religion *of* Jesus but also that which centers *about* him, and which lies in our unconscious *if* we are Protestants.

The "Jesus cults" among young people, especially in the communes, the popular musical success of "Jesus Christ Superstar" and "rock" church services as almost religious drama to youth, all show the need for a fresh look at Jesus in relation to the Christ image, and how Jesus did not identify with it. The appeal of the popular projections of Christ onto Jesus shows that those involved in such movements have yet to come to terms with the Jesus of the Synoptics, and yet desire him. The great interest in Jesus Christ among the so-called Jesus "Freaks" represent a different kind but just as strong a projection as to Jesus as the traditional one. Turning to the Orient and discarding the archetype of our Western religious heritage may indicate the resistance to facing substance and darkness but may also reflect a need to get back to more inclusiveness. Many young people who turn to the East are positive about the "bliss, light, joy, no head-trip" attitude they want to find. But man needs to really get related to the depth of his own heritage before turning to the East. And few are willing to pay the price for growth in either tradition.

We have much to learn from the East, but if such learning is to be authentic and not a substitute, it must be used by us after we have rootedness in our own religious culture. I see many people in analysis looking for values in eastern systems (and rightly so), but something is unhealthy if these values are grafted on, or over, certain splits and neuroses that are a part of Western religion. Whether we like it or not we are Christians and Jews, some of both. We cannot pretend to be other. A Buddhist image or symbol may be a central picture on which to meditate; one may use it *just because* it does not have the connotation of a Christ picture. But also one has to know why one does or does not respond to the great Christian artists, from Giotto to Roualt.

The term *imitatio Christi* can be very negative if used as meaning an attempt to be like Jesus. It may be very negative if generalized so that "Christ" includes any Savior figure. But it may be very positive if seen as a challenge to be fully and completely oneself, as Jesus was himself, having found that Self through the acceptance of diverse elements within the personality, including not only the shadow negative elements but also those religious or spiritual forces which are part of our heritage, unredeemed and unused through repression and lack of assimilation. The price for discovery of these elements is a great price — not easy and not for all. But I believe that the great chance we have as Protestants, and the only chance that the Protestant church has to meet the present spiritual and psychic needs of its parishioners, is the daring to confront the universal inner forces (the archetypes) and to learn to express and channel them in one's own unique way, thereby living one's own personality. This does not sound too daring – but to risk being an Individual, not an individualist, is hazardous and unpopular.

Let me end with another dream of a modern man: "I was buying some things in a market. One of the treasures was a pearl. The man told me the price but I couldn't yet afford it. However, I knew that eventually I would and could pay the price." When we, too, learn not only that the attainment of the pearl of great price involves a change of conscious attitude (which it surely does) but that a bit of the universal pearl is in our unconscious depths, to be realized there, then our Protestant dilemma will be solved. Then we may once again be grasped and transformed by a Reality which is not of our making, which is not to be understood only by our mind nor felt by our emotions, but which moves at the core of our Being if we will make the journey to arrive there. And when we get there, at the point of finding ourselves, we may be able to say, as T.S. Eliot says in *Four Quartettes:*

> What we call the beginning is often the end
> And to make an end is to make a beginning.
> The end is where we start from.
> We shall not cease our exploration
> And the end of all our exploring
> Will be to arrive where we started
> And to know the place for the first time.

Note: Two points need to be added. Since the delivery of this paper, there have been revolutionary developments in both the Protestant and Catholic churches and a more recent paper of mine on the *Symbolism behind Liturgy, Creed and Prayer* will be published this coming winter and will, in one sense, bring this whole subject more up to date.

ANALYTICAL PSYCHOLOGY AND THE SYNOPTIC GOSPELS

I have never forgotten a statement made by Dr. Henry B. Sharman, the New Testament scholar with whom I worked. In commenting on William James' book, *Varieties of Religious Experience*, Dr. Sharman said, "It is indeed strange that the most wholesome religious experience in history is omitted, as it always is; namely, the experience of Jesus himself." Neglect of the experience of Jesus has long characterized the field of Christian theology and history. Christianity has been and is a religion *about* Jesus or Jesus Christ. It has centered on the individual's experience of Christ as Saviour rather than on the relationship of the man Jesus to God. Christian dogma, especially the dogma of the incarnation, has been the focal point of religion. The human catalyst has been forgotten. The reasons for this are both understandable and natural, but perhaps the time has come for a corrective evaluation.

Analytical Psychology, in its research into religious and psychological reality, has provided the most comprehensive and satisfactory explanation of the meaning of Christian dogma, and the experiences behind it, through an understanding of the archetypes. It has given us the possibility of interpreting such dogma on a psychological-mythological basis. It has unlocked for us something of the mystery without destroying the mystery. But Analytical Psychology, too, has neglected the experient Jesus of the Synoptic Gospels (Matthew, Mark and Luke) as a genuine human contributor to the development of religious consciousness. The book of Revelation, the book of the Acts, the Fourth Gospel, the Old Testament, as well as the richness of the heretical sects of Gnosticism and Alchemy, are all objects of study and analysis, as well they should be. However, the material in the Synoptic Gospels has not been properly considered.

Analytical Psychology has observed and worked with the empirical fact that the Self may be symbolized in the Christ-figure, and has emphasized that the meaning of the Christ image must be discovered by the individual. In the area of impersonal-historical evaluation and progression, Analytical Psychology has been concerned with the new archetype which was constellated at the time of Jesus and which then captured the Mediterranean world. One of Jung's greatest contributions has been to point out that the ultimate reality of God could, in part, be reflected in the archetype and could, therefore, be better grasped by men. In trying to understand Christianity as a new form, a new birth, a shattering of old patterns, it has been natural to leave out the person of Jesus. This remains true regardless of whether one sees Christianity entirely as a new revelation or as part of an historical continuum. Yet by this omission, is it not possible that Analytical Psychology has made somewhat the same mistake that Christianity made – that is, to equate the experience of Jesus and the experience about the projections *upon* Jesus as Savior? If the experiences are *not* the same–and I believe they are not–then many questions must be asked and answered. In his book, *Answer to Job*, for instance, Dr. Jung *almost* seems to equate the dogmatic Christ and the person of Jesus, and thus the God of the Christian incarnation and the God to whom Jesus was related. (I say, "almost", because after personal conversation with him, I think this is not entirely true.) But, actually, are they the same? If not, how did the shift occur and why? Are there different levels of Godhead and its incarnation? And, very centrally, what relation did Jesus have to the dark side of God not included in the Christian picture? I believe Dr. Jung is right in his concern about the over-emphasis on the light side in the Christian picture. At the same time, I believe that what Jesus himself emphasized was not only light.

Before approaching these questions, let me say a few fundamental things about myths and archetypes. All of these ideas may be known to those who are aware of and experienced in Analytical Psychology. Nevertheless, they may give a better point from which to look at the complex subject before us.

All of the great myths of mankind express in concrete form the longing of man to understand himself and his inner and outer universe. They are expressions of the activity of the archetype of the Self at different levels of consciousness. They are patterns of how man images himself and his development, forms of the interaction between man and the cosmic, supra-personal powers. The hero-myth is one specific form of religious-psychological myth that concerns itself with man's journey to free himself from unconscious domination. It is always about a journey, a way to be followed. That way is characterized by difficulties and obstacles to be overcome; there is attendant suffering; there are helpful creatures as well as regressive pulls. The hero is committed to follow the forces of destiny which operate in his life. Only by "dying to himself" can he be aware of and respond to the wisdom that is other than his own. Great hero-myths, from the Babylonian Gilgamesh to the American Indian Self-Teacher, express the struggle for wholeness through traversing the way. The archetypes in the mythic patterns may change colour from culture to culture. The patterns of the myth also may change, very slowly, as the consciousness of man changes and grows. One may say that each time a new level of myth is expressed, a new phase has been concretized in cultural evolution, and a new kind of incarnation has occurred. What, after all, is the meaning of "incarnation" other than a bringing into the flesh, into reality, into manifestation, into time, that which is eternal, beyond time, supra-human? The hero incarnates that to which he is devoted; the nature of the hero and that to which he is devoted changes as consciousness changes.

The heroes of mankind are of two sorts. There are, first, those individuals on whom collective society projects the hero myth. These are not necessarily the real heroes because they have not necessarily travelled the hero's road. For example, there are the various negative or positive political figures, such as Hitler, Roosevelt, Lincoln or Gandhi. The sources of this tendency to mythologize history are much better understood through the theories of Analytical Psychology than through sociological theory. Secondly, there are those few individuals who do in very truth actually live out the struggle for wholeness, whether on a modest or a grand scale. These are the real heroes at any period of history. They bring the myth to life, they realize it in time and place. Possibly most of the great turning points of history are times when the inner archetype of God and the nature of consciousness in man are together ready for a new convulsive step of development. A new hero must appear at these times.

Such a moment was evidently present in the Judaic-Roman world at the time of the coming of Christianity. What happened then is what inevitably happens at such moments. Through projection, these true heroes become the heroes for others and are, therefore, robbed of their own heroic natures. They arouse the central Self in others, but instead of it being lived out consciously by these others, it is projected. So it is that Jesus became the hero to others, became identified, by a process we shall try to explain, with the Christ image and the Self. He became the centre of the frame, the object of religious devotion. What he taught and lived became distorted and temporarily or permanently lost. What the original impulse of God was that moved in the man and to which the man responded could not yet be received by people, and a deviant aspect was stressed. Why the Jewish people at that time did not make the fundamental projection, but rather rejected Jesus, and why the non-Jewish world did accept him, at least as they understood him through Paul, has not been fully answered. This centering on Jesus Christ proved adequate then, as it contained the mass of the people and thus remained functional. Today it seems not to be so, and for many of us it seems not to fulfill either the need of man or of God. It has led many erstwhile Christians to reject religion, to say that God is dead. It has led that outstanding theologian, the late Dr. Paul Tillich, to ask whether or not Christianity is "irrelevant".

There is a further possibility, however, for Jew and Christian alike. This is to look with fresh eyes on the Synoptic story of the man who really lived in his time and place, and in that story to see what is manifested. My own conviction is that an historical-critical study of the three Synoptic gospels, by which one can get behind the

Christian accretions and editorial comments to something authentic, is truly possible. One can do it only by the greatest devotion to open-mindedness, and by the pursuit of a scientific investigation that takes one beyond Christian bias. If one does this, there is revealed an experient of religious reality, the man Jesus, confronted by the *numinous* and spending his brief life attempting to express it, to relate to it, but never to identify with it. Jesus attempted to be as conscious an individual as possible in relating himself and others to his own revelation of God. The tone of the fourth gospel, exemplified by "the Father and I are one", is wholly absent from the Synoptic accounts, where one finds such statements as "Why callest thou me good?" (Mark 10:18), and "Not everyone that saith unto me, 'Lord, Lord,' shall enter the kingdom of heaven" (Matt. 7:21). He related to the Source but never became it.

Jesus was well aware of the messianic or Christ image held at that time by the Jews. Did he identify himself with that image? What was his messianic self-consciousness? Did he see himself as others, especially the disciples, saw him? And what was his relation to the enigmatic phrase, "Son of man," found frequently in the gospels, but nowhere else in the New Testament, found originally in Enoch, Ezekiel and Daniel?

It seems immediately evident that this person of Jesus is far from the idealistic ethical reformer of much of liberal Protestantism. This nice but uninteresting image of him has indeed been a further reason for the neglect of Jesus as individual. Rather we must see him as dynamically relating to the moving archetype of his time.

Before returning to these questions, it may be relevant to add a word of the experience out of which I write this paper, and to state its limitations. I present these tentative conclusions only secondarily out of my many years of experience as a Jungian analyst. They come primarily out of my experience of conducting seminars for more than thirty years in the Synoptic Gospels and observing the impact of this material on people, some of whom have and some of whom have not had analysis. Although my seminar work began immediately following university, with intensive study with Dr. Henry B. Sharman, an outstanding New Testament scholar who conducted such seminars, I must state, with no false humility, that, because of limitation of time due to professional practice, I cannot pretend to be a New Testament scholar.

In the seminars I have led for many years the attempt has been made to help people, by a non-authoritative question and discussion method, to make a comparative study of the first three gospels for the purpose of understanding better the consciousness of Jesus. The material in the gospels which may be considered as coming from Jesus has been centrally considered; but other non-historical material indicative of the trends of the time, or later additions, have been given as much time as possible. It is extremely difficult for people even to begin to ask questions about the inner world that Jesus confronted. We Christians have literally never taken him, his achievement, and his consciousness seriously. The fact that there are three gospels in a literary relationship of interdependence has made such research possible. This is the fundamental basis of all New Testament research. What has distinguished our seminars has been willingness to try to be objective about subjective biases, in the search for the truth of what actually is there in the records. The method is really comparable to the amplification method used in dream-analysis, with contributions from all participants. My own interest in Analytical Psychology came as a result of Synoptic study and of the need to enlarge my understanding of human personality.

Let me raise some of the kinds of questions I raise in seminars. What kind of a man was Jesus of Nazareth? What did he stress? What was his effect on others? Most basically, how did he get his insights, and from where? Relative to where he found his insight, his gnosis, his wisdom, I try to include both the historical roots of it and also his personal experience, as the two conditioning factors. The *Dead Sea Scrolls* are shedding valuable new light on the historical milieu which formed the background of Jesus. Even from the briefest acquaintance with the research on them, it seems apparent that the Scrolls, especially the *Manual of the Community of the New Covenant*, give information on the activities of a group either identified with or close to the Essenes. Their founder, the Master of Justice, the Teacher of Righteousness, who lived about fifty years before Jesus, and was martyred, had many similarities to and many differences from the later prophet. The rules of life and conduct of this group had much in common with the forms of the early Christian community. The Dead Sea Scrolls may be a shock to those who see the Christian revelation not as historically rooted, but as a break in the organic growth of consciousness, and thus utterly unique. To those of us with a different standpoint, such data on certain trends with Judaic thought (and Judaic mysticism) should be deeply accepted.

Jesus was a man whose whole concern was the reign of God in people's lives. *That* is not new. It describes all the prophets of the Old Testament. But there is every indication that Jesus expressed a new level of the meaning and character both of God's role and of man's role in the achievement of consciousness. He knew, although he would have stated it in other words, that God manifested Himself in the Self. He knew the inwardness of reality, as expressed in "your Father which seeth in secret" (Matt. 5:4), or "the Kingdom of God is within" (Luke 17:2). He taught in all the parables on the Kingdom of God that growth was quiet, inward, unspectacular, mysterious and dynamic. He knew the transcendent was there to become immanent.

And he knew, I believe, that to achieve creative inwardness man must know and accept himself in his totality. No point in the teaching of Jesus is more at variance with most Christian teaching than that of self-acceptance. We know too well the repressive, one-sided religious emphasis on the light, on the masculine rather than the feminine, on the concern for perfection instead of wholeness. It might be enlightening to mention a few passages from the Gospels which have to do with Jesus' outlook on man, his knowledge of man's shadow, his non-condemnatory acceptance of totality and the subsequent necessary transformation. He says, "Resist not evil" (Matt. 5:39). This is usually interpreted only outwardly, instead of being seen in its inward implication. No "evil" in the psyche is met and dealt with by resistance, but rather by openness, by giving the other cheek, by taking a compassionate, maternal attitude whereby transformation can take place. This is very different from the condemnatory "Thou shalt not," and requires a much higher degree of consciousness.

He said to love both the neighbour and the enemy. He does not say there is no enemy, which would be much easier; rather, he says that we must include our enemies, because that is the way God Himself acts. We are created in His image and, as He has opposites within Himself, so have we, and attention must be paid to both sides. It is at the end of the passage about loving both sides, including the enemy, that Jesus says, "Ye therefore shall be perfect as your heavenly Father is perfect" (Matt. 5:48). There is reputable alternative reading which says, "Ye therefore shall be all-inclusive as God is all-inclusive." Usually perfectionism for us does not mean all-inclusiveness. Although we do not often interpret his statement in the Old Testament manner of "hate your enemy," we do pretend that the enemy is not the enemy, that the dark opponent is, after all, really light.

In that remarkable scene with the Pharisees and sinners at dinner, Jesus evidently prefers to eat with the sinners, those shadow elements who stand opposite to the rigid conservatives. He not only likes them, but feels they have far more hope for salvation. Why? Because Jesus sensed that it is these very shadow elements in men which lie closer to the Self and are the stuff out of which redemption comes. Jesus knew the split in man, and he knew what aspect held the potential for change.

Let us examine the parable of the Good Samaritan, in its inner as well as its outer meaning (Luke 10:25-37). (And perhaps it is a sign of great consciousness in Jesus that it is possible to let his images apply both ways.) When we are in trouble, who is our neighbour, according to Jesus? It is not the priest or Levite, but the Samaritan, the one most hated by the status-quo side, who comes to protect and rescue. Our neighbour is not the one we would have expected, the one closest to us, but rather the one who is farthest from us. And the parable of the Prodigal Son (the closest story we have in the Gospels to a myth of the whole journey) states that only out of utmost darkness and loss and despair do we "come to ourselves" (Luke 15:11-32).

What better statement of the split in the psyche has ever been made than in the famous condemnation of the Pharisees in the "Woes" (Matt. 23)? Here Jesus describes aspects of man most tellingly in addressing the Pharisee in man, the arrogant, proud, egocentric element making "clean the outside of the cup," building the "whited sepulchre," "attending to the tithing of the mint and anise and cumin," yet inwardly being full of "extortion and excess," "of dead men's bones," and leaving unattended the "weightier matters of mercy and faith". Jesus shows he knew that defilement comes from within, from these "beams" which the individual would rather project on others.

All of this is a most re-creative approach after much of the Christian teaching of "shoulds, oughts and don'ts". And Jesus, although he has strong words to say about anger and sex, never presents an ethic based on repression and lack of recognition – rather an ethic based on the reality of personality at a very down-to-earth level. That this made his morality more difficult to follow is self-evident.

It is in no sense new or unique to say that Jesus honoured the individual and placed responsibility on him. But there are many levels of meaning in the individual. I think it questionable whether Jesus knew of individuation in the more specific definition of that term as given by Dr. Jung. But he does assert that there is an element in man to be trusted, a center to be achieved, a new man to be born through responsibility and transformation. No better examples can be seen than in Mark 2:1-28, in four outstanding instances where he asserts the necessity of individual decision based on consciousness. First is the scene with the palsied man, where forgiveness is defined as the ability to start again, to assert freedom of will, and to act as if nothing were being held against one; second is the instance already referred to of the Pharisees and sinners; third is the incident where the disciples are accused of not fasting, and Jesus answers that man must fast when he feels a need and desire, and not on the basis of collective rules; and fourth is the similar situation when Jesus states the relation between man and the Sabbath. It is in relation to this last incident that the non-canonical statement, "Blessed art thou if thou knowest what thou doest," appears. Jesus calls on the individual to grow and develop by using his natural talents, not by repressing them. The parable on the hidden talent (Matt. 25:14-28) is an excellent illustration of this emphasis.

What is this individual whom Jesus felt could be trusted? Was it the "unredeemed" natural man who would go out and do what he wanted, or was it a "redeemed" man? If Jesus stressed the dark side of human nature as well as the light side, he also stressed that there was a way of life, a way of integration whereby man could become trustful and trusted. Jesus taught a way wherein man became a son to the Father who was always there, waiting and needing and helping the son to be begotten. It did not matter when one started this work. The workers at the eleventh hour received the same as those who came earlier (Matt. 20:1-6). This way involved the discovery (and Jesus articulated it in a remarkably lucid manner) of a fundamentally spiritual law which involved a new level of God-man relationship. From the standpoint of God, it offered a new possibility of God being born in man. From the standpoint of man, the Father was both beyond man yet in man as co-creator. The son was also part of each individual because each must work to produce the outcome. The further implication of this as to the role of the Holy Spirit leads toward the concept of the Trinity. Man, through his voluntary commitment to transformation, could find a supra-natural center from which decision and action could stem. There is one element about this law in the Gospels, however, which seems to have escaped the notice of most people. If Jesus stated a hard way of transformation to be followed, he also *always* stated, in broad, rich and provocative terms, where that way would lead. He pointed out that whenever the way is taken as conscious responsibility, a result or reward follows. It is evident that this concept contains the idea of initiation as found in the mystery religions and in the great Gnostic teachings. For example:

> If one enters the narrow gate, one will find life. (Matt. 7:13).
>
> If one loses one's live, one finds it (Mark 8:35).
>
> If one does the will of God, one has eternal life. (Luke 10:25-28).
>
> If one sells all, one enters the Kingdom of God. (Matt. 3:45-46).
>
> If one's eye is single, one's whole body is full of light (Luke 11:34).

These two halves are never divorced in any statement I know of in the Gospels. This does not mean that one will always know the specific results at once. The Navaho Indian statement, "We shall know where we are going when we get there," applies very precisely here. Jesus stressed that one never knows where one's loyalty will lead, for the ways of God are indeed mysterious. Perhaps it is true that "few be they that find it" (Matt. 7:14), and that to be elected or to hear this "call to vocation," as Jung has termed it, is a destiny fraught at once with privilege and with hardship. But that this way of initiation is always worthwhile, albeit crucifying, is part of the teaching of Jesus.

If man is to serve the demands of God as manifested within as well as without, to serve through ego choices, what else can be said about the concept of God? Jesus saw

God, as did many of the Old Testament figures, as a numinous element making for wholeness to be obeyed and followed. He called God's will purposiveness or direction; yet in essence this will was a-moral, waiting for man to make it moral. That God *was*, and was purposive, was not new. But for Jesus, God and man were ready to attempt manifestation at a new level. If God was more ready to become conscious, Jesus knew the level of totality of commitment which a man must have so that nothing of himself was left out in helping God to evolve. The God of Jesus included emphasis on both masculine and feminine, on spirit and substance, on both the light and dark sides, on conscious and unconscious. In speaking earlier of inwardness, I stressed what I felt to be the newest focal point; namely, that Jesus saw God as manifest in creatureliness and humanness. The gap between God and man could be healed by each person at this more inclusive level of development. This was what Jesus would have meant by incarnation, and by very definition it is feminine in substance, as opposed to the purely masculine spirit. One cannot stress too often that Jesus was not a Christian. Nor was he an orthodox Jew. Just what he emerged as, as a new third, becomes a vital point. The greatest statement of Jesus, the only one that has a three-document tradition, (Mark, Doc. P. and the Gospel of John), "Whosoever shall lose his life shall save it" (Luke 17:33), places the highest value on the psyche as the container of divinity. It might read, in a free rendering, "Whosoever will allow the rigid boundaries around his own psyche to drop, will find a vitality of life inside."

It has seemed evident to me for a long time that no person could have used such rich feminine symbolism as one sees in the parables, or expressed so many eros attitudes of love and relationship, unless he had deeply touched the feminine side of himself and God. That Jesus stressed the spirit side because of his cultural heritage and its needs, I would never deny. But I cannot believe that his Yahweh had, so to speak, parted company with Sophia! Rather the wisdom element was implicit but central. The Jewish mystical idea of the Shekinah was possibly significant in the thought of Jesus. At least one can say that a great contribution of Jesus was to raise the dark feminine side of nature to the level of Agape.

Let me now return to the question of the dark or unconscious side of God, which Dr. Jung discusses in his *Answer to Job*. I have never doubted that, for Jesus, God was to be feared as well as loved, in the sense that one never knew ahead of time what were His demands, and they were often not "good" as we define "good". The "will of God" was not good except in the broad sense that by following it one came to Life. He is also to be feared because His wrath is there in the process if we do not follow the creative way. This is most exemplified in the parable of the wise and foolish virgins (Mt. 25:1-12) where the door is shut on the foolish, and in the parable (Mt. 25:14-28) on the use of the talents where the Lord is wrathful with the servant who does not use his capacities to the full. Both these parables, and others, remind one of Jacob Boehme's definition of God as the "Nothing that wants to become Something" and is wrathful if we do not help Him so to become.

God is also to be feared not only because of His threat to our egocentric point of view, but because He has within Himself the regressive Satanic side, not wanting to be conscious. This opposition creates the positive tension under which we live. The phrase in the Lord's Prayer, "Lead us not into temptation" (Luke 11:4), may be one of affirmation in the light of fundamental realities. Thus it could read: "May I not be pulled by deep unconsciousness which is in my nature and Yours." The temptation to do so is there. It is the human predicament. I am in it. But my prayer is to remain loyal to consciousness because that is what is needed on both sides. I think that this is more consistent with the beautiful parable which follows the prayer (Luke 11:5-8). This parable describes a man who has a friend coming at midnight for food. But the man has no food, so he goes to another friend who has a source of supply. But this second friend is loathe to get up and get the bread, being comfortable in bed with his children. Yet because of the first man's importunity, the possessor of bread finally does get up and give him a loaf. This is to say that, because the ego, the conscious side, has kept loyal to its need to feed the whole, the Self responded. Is this not the picture of the nature of the ambivalent God, the source of all supply? On the one hand, He does not want to wake up, to become conscious, to give the bread. Yet through man's persistence, He finally does arouse Himself. Is it not perhaps the negative feminine side that most resists consciousness? Is not the part that is asleep, the unillumined part, demanding greater consciousness from us in order to be aroused and redeemed?

What can we say about the sources of Jesus' awareness? Out of what personally did his insight come, as distinct from all the historical circumstances impinging on him? Of course, in the last analysis it is an unanswerable question as to what he was totally like, due to the confusion of history and myth. But I believe that this does not relieve us from seeing as much as we can from the recorded history. The accounts of his baptism and wilderness experiences may be determinative in illuminating all we have been dealing with, and may help us to see why his life led to the cross and to what happened afterwards.

Jesus joined the movement of John the Baptist and underwent the baptismal rite symbolic of what the Baptist called "repentance" and "remission of sins". He went into the water, and, emerging, experienced "the spirit as a dove" descending. He saw the "heavens rent asunder," and heard a voice calling him "beloved son" (Mark 1:10-11). These are the reported words. It seems realistic to assume they came from Jesus as a symbolic description to others of the experience, because certainly the experience resulted in genuine changes in him and his life. If this had only been a later archetypal projection by someone else, the rest of the story would make no sense. But it does. The baptism is the conscious choice of a man facing his own myth.

What does it mean? How was Jesus different after the baptismal experience? One could say that he met the challenge of John's movement and went into the inner world with such devotion and intensity that he had a fundamental experience of knowing the God within as well as without, the Other, the numinous. This experience of being grasped was felt as receiving the spirit. Two features seem particularly meaningful in the light of later emphasis. One is the matter of direction. Jesus goes down and re-emerges. Today we would say that he found spirit in substance. A new aspect of the Self was born at that moment; the spirit found a new dwelling place. Surely this determines his later stress on inwardness. The other feature is the spirit "as a dove," the bird of Venus and Aphrodite, not the masculine Logos. Two pairs of opposites have been constellated, the up and the down, the feminine and the masculine. The feminine is seen in the symbols of water, descent, and dove; the masculine in the ascent, heaven, spirit and the voice. Also, the use of the phrase "beloved son" might well be the lightening of a new birth. At a minimum, Jesus felt a sense of affirmation, felt the rightness of his choice. Awareness of the Father-son relationship was not new, but what kind of a relationship did this experience imply? It had within it the possibility of that special form of functioning central to the Jews, the messianic function. It could have meant that he felt himself to be the special one sent for the redemption of his people, the anointed one, to serve either politically or in some other way. In archetypal terms, the messianic hope seems to me to be the hope of the Self projected on to a mediator outside. It is important to be aware of the specific forms of Jewish expectations, or nothing later in the teaching of Jesus is clear. Did Jesus here consider himself as being the Messiah or Christ; did he see himself in those terms? If he experienced the reality of the Self at the highest and deepest level of consciousness, and if sonship describes that, it could well have taken a messianic form of call to vocation. If he experienced salvation or rebirth and vocation, could he naturally entertain the idea of messiahship which many others also had at that time?

With all this in his heart and mind, Jesus goes to the wilderness for a long period of time. He goes to aloneness, to the inwardly and outwardly unexplored, to ponder on the meaning of the demands of his God on him. How should he use the power, the new perception? In this struggle another pair of opposites, the beasts and the angels, the instinctual and spiritual elements within, are helpful and "with" him.

The general framework of what happened in the wilderness is well known. Jesus rejected (Matt. 4:1-11) three so-called temptations attributed to Satan, rejected three different kinds of leadership – political, miraculous, and economic. "This and this and this" are not the ways the Kingdom of God will be brought in. What is all too often overlooked, because taken so for granted in Christianity, is that Jesus is acting in a highly conscious way, struggling with deep archetypal images of his people. He is being decisive. And it is also overlooked that the images, the forms of activity, which he temporarily considers but then rejects, are central, sacred, deeply-cherished concepts of his people. He is cutting through all orthodox religious expectations, and one cannot fail to be moved by the courageous awareness of this human being.

The crucial problem of Satan needs now to be explored briefly. Rather than seeing Satan as Christianity has, as representing an autonomous evil aspect luring Jesus away from God's will, with the attendant assumption of duality and split, I see Jesus struggling with a Satanic principle as an inner aspect or facet of God pushing him into great consciousness. Here is no duality, but a man confronted by possibilities within the nature of God. Jesus labels these elements Satanic after he has rejected them. We must see that the proposals by Satan are collectively held, positive, "good" images. Jesus' great consciousness consists in coming from the baptism to face the images which seemed God's will to his people, in being able to make a choice of a new undefined form, and then in calling these other images Satanic.

This is a subtle but significant progression. God and Satan here are two aspects of a whole – and after Jesus rejects collective images he can see them as Satanic because they are unconscious. The material hope for a Messiah is a lure from the dark side of God. The opposite hope of individual consciousness is there in God and manifest in

Jesus. He is separating out and discriminating between elements within the archetype itself. That both sides appear as parts of God is the first indication we have that he knew both sides. (I might add here that I see some of the experiences described in Revelation not only as the dark, autonomous anti-Christ expressing itself because of repression by the later Christian attitude, but perhaps as a regression after the individual forward movement made by Jesus.) It is much easier to split the archetype apart and make a duality than to tolerate the ambiguity of God in His two aspects. By rejecting the current concepts of Judaic Messianism Jesus changes and alters the content of the Christ image. He frees it from its external forms and internalizes it. He brings it as an inner mediating force. In this sense he rejects the limitation of the Jewish aspect but maintains the central positive values. This act of bringing the Christ-image back within the psyche to its genesis or origin fundamentally altered the archetype of the God-man relationship. How much the concepts of Jewish mysticism or of the mystery religions influenced Jesus may not be known until further discoveries are made. Here I am concerned only to show that he dealt directly with the Christ or messianic image out of his experience with John the Baptist. Whatever one's evaluation of it, the historical fact is that the later Christians used Jesus as symbol and the Jewish people rejected him as symbol.

How, then, as a result of this, did Jesus see himself? He constantly turned people's attention to God, not to himself. He discriminated sharply between himself, as human, and the Holy Spirit within. In that significant passage on blasphemy (Mt. 12:32), he says in effect, "Say what you want to about me, but not about the Holy Spirit in me." He never doubted himself as a channel, but he always escaped inflation and arrogance which come from identification. Most important, he never accepted or affirmed himself as the Messiah or Christ, yet he never denied it, which presents a genuine enigma. The only passage about the trials where there is a clear-cut "I am" answer (Mark 14:61) is probably not authentic, because at this point Matthew has the ambiguous "Thou sayest" (Matt. 26:64). In the light of Matthew's whole apologia, he would never have missed a chance to put in the "I am" if it had been there. What does it mean if Jesus never accepted the messianic title? It could reflect precisely what happened in the wilderness– the refusal of specific Judaic forms. What does it mean, on the other hand, that he never denied it by a flat "No"? This could mean that inwardly he did relate to the meaning of the Christ image and knew it as a present numinous factor in the psyche of each man. He did not identify himself with it as later Christianity did. He did not say he *was it*, but he could never deny it as real and alive because it was exactly what he had touched. And because he had touched it, he aroused wholeness in others who projected it on him.

The designation "Son of man" is one which, I believe, Jesus did use about a principle within himself, as well as one which also later was attributed to him. (See the separate paper in this volume called *Son of Man, Expression of the Self).* This has been a puzzling phrase to New Testament scholars. It seems to be used in the Gospels as meaning either I, Jesus, as man in a special but not unique way, or I, Jesus, as Messiah. The first meaning is found in passages which seem to be authentic, and the second in passages which are probably later accretions. If, as Dr. Jung points out in *Answer to Job*, we have anticipations in Ezekiel, Enoch and Daniel of an archetype of God's approach to man, of God's incarnation in man, may it be that Jesus used "Son of man" at this new level of meaning? That is, did his use of it carry out the original hints about it? (This would need to be distinguished from possible messianic interpretations of the phrase which were attributed to him.) To illustrate this point, let me give two instances. In Mark 2:27-28, Jesus speaks of the Sabbath being made for man, and therefore he says, the "Son of man is lord even of the Sabbath." At this point both Matthew and Luke, as copyists, omit the reference to the Sabbath being made for man, and include only "The Son of man is lord even of the Sabbath." This can only be accounted for by their wanting to put Jesus in an exclusive, unique, possibly messianic position. In the original statement in Mark, I would assume Jesus is using the phrase to designate a divine quality within man on which man's individuality is based. It is not synonymous with man, and it is not the Self in its ultimate meaning. It is somewhere in between. One senses the same meaning in the passage already referred to about blasphemy, where Jesus says that one may say what one wants to against the Son of man, but not against the Holy Spirit. Is it possible that the Son of man and the Holy Spirit are the two sides of the Self, one facing toward the human, and the other facing toward the God beyond?

The question as to whether the more specifically apocalyptic passages referring to the Son of man (Mark 13:26), which came originally from the Old Testament, were part of the thought of Jesus, is one about which I do not feel sure. I feel confident that specific references to his own "coming again" were later attributed to Jesus. But it is not inconceivable that Jesus shared with his people some idea of a final "Day" to come.

It is possibly clearer now why the preaching of the "good tidings" of the possibility of individual responsibility and redemption, not through either the law or through belief as preached by later Christianity, led Jesus to Gethsemane and the cross. His emphasis, morally and spiritually, cut through all current collective standards. The phrase of Kierkegaard, "the alarming possibility of being able," seems a dramatic way of saying what Jesus was teaching.

In Gethsemane we have a supreme moment of human achievement. On the one hand, Jesus exhibits complete open-ness, readiness, and loyalty to the demands of God and eternity and the fulfillment of destiny. On the other hand, there is the human acknowledgment of limitation and desire, "If it be possible, remove this cup from me" (Mark 14:36). This is the paradox of prayer to bring the human in fullness of desire, and yet hold it in abeyance before whatever total demand may be made. This daring affirmation of the desire to live and the question of right choice (is it or is it not God's will that he die) saves Jesus from a martyr's resignation and a death which would have been a much lesser, a much easier death. By contrast, the disciples cannot sustain the tension, succumb to sleep, and give way to the unconscious.

For Jesus the experient, the cross, whatever it later means to us, was completion, finality, what he had earlier called being "perfected" (Luke 13:32). It represented the utmost loyalty to the principle of consciousness. And it was darkness for him because it released the imperfection and unconsciousness of man, foreshadowed in such poignant passages as Luke 13:34: "O Jerusalem, Jerusalem, which killeth the prophets and stoneth them that are sent unto her!" Moreover, it was the darkness that came from taking full responsibility for the task of being human, thus changing the nature of God. "My God, my God, why hast Thou forsaken me?" (Mark 15:34) may be the utterance of a man in utter agony, a man who knows that, at this moment, God can do nothing because man has channelled His, God's, power into consciousness and therefore reduced God's omnipotence.

Why had the crucifixion to come? Because the dark, unconscious elements in Jesus' world were threatened by his totality and consciousness, by his challenge of inclusiveness, and he was nailed to the cross by them. The shadow, the evil elements which he embraced as part of God and man seemed to have triumphed at that moment of total darkness described so vividly in Matthew 27:45-51. Throughout the story a few disciples were present with their ambivalent attitudes towards Jesus. They responded to him, never leaving him (not even Peter, despite his denials, went away). They partly understood him, preached what he taught them—and at the same time they were egocentric, petty, putting images of expectation on him, wanting him to fulfill their needs, not his. At his death all the hopes, the longings, the wishes for him to be their Messiah, must have fallen to utter ruin. One cannot imagine what darkness must have been theirs when their leader went. Much could be said about the inner symbolic meaning of Gethsemane and the cross. Is not Jesus here the embodiment of the Self at its highest conscious level—awake, alert, insightful, and filled with suffering because the cross has been voluntarily chosen? (The disciples are always present in us, too, as the sleeping, unconscious parts, not yet transformed, never forsaking the garden but never fully related.) Three times Jesus approaches them—three, a number of tension and restlessness. Just because of their projection on him, they cannot arise and act independently until they lose him. The very rich symbolism of the cross with the two thieves, the women at the foot of the cross, the stigmata, the soldiers, the man Jesus on the cross, all constitute a rich mandala brought into history.

At the point of the crucifixion something happened. The disciples, a few or all of them, underwent a crucial spiritual re-birth out of darkness, wherein they touched the inward God and felt the new life stirring in the abyss. The very thing which Jesus had been preaching and living—the resurrected life—which had never been quite grasped by them because of his presence in reality, now took hold of them. This new presence, however, was felt to be not the presence of God, but of Jesus. He was no longer dead but alive, they felt. The "resurrection" was their new life sensed as his presence in living reality. The experience of God taking hold of them was interpreted by them as Jesus reborn. So Christianity, as we have known it for two thousand years, came into being. The man Jesus became the symbol to carry the religious meaning. If Jesus was alive after all, the disciples could project on to him their hope for him to come again. This hope at first took on a more current Jewish flavour and then later was attributed to Jesus. I believe this accounts for most of the eschatological passages of his coming again, such as found in Matthew 10:23. Within a short time, this precise form of Christology changed, but the fundamental symbolic treatment remained. Even in the experience of Pentecost, where the projection was more internalized, the symbol focussed on Jesus as Christ. I am convinced that neither this Pentecostal Christ concept nor the experience of the disciples was part of the experience of Jesus as Jew. The disciples simply *had* to carry it forward in a different form. But because the forms that have been central to Christianity are undergoing such changes today, the original experience of Jesus may become the more relevant.

One psychological need is for a deeper understanding of what were the factors underlying the Jewish non-acceptance of both Jesus and Christianity. It is very easy to say that, of course, people today would do the same thing, but that sidesteps the historical problem. Aside from the archetypal motif of the redemptive coming out of the rejected, thus making rejection inevitable, there are two other possibilities. Did the very rigidity of the Jewish concept concerning the form of the work of the Messiah prevent the Jewish people both from understanding Jesus' change of emphasis to the inner, and also from accepting the disciples' experience? Secondly, did the emphasis in Jewish thought on the masculine make too difficult the idea of inclusion of the Substance, the feminine?

Another question arising from the historical-psychological development must be raised. What happened to the message of Jesus when, under Paul's influence, it went beyond the frontiers of Palestine and met the Graeco-Roman world? Some of what was preached did conform to the teaching of Jesus. But the idea of "belief" in him, and the tendency to be concerned only with the "light" side, led to repression of most other elements intrinsic in the psychology of Jesus. These emphases, while making a strong and justifiable appeal to a degenerate Roman World, complicated the Jewish attitude towards Jesus. For the very genius of Jewish religion which flowered in Jesus was lost. Jesus and the Gospels were forgotten by Christian and Jew alike. Further work is involved in tracing how Jesus' message moved when it came in contact with the rest of the world, when it encountered both Greek philosophy and Gnosticism, thus leading to the Fourth Gospel, to Revelations, and to the final formulation of Christian dogma.

Let me conclude with a summary of what I believe to be the greatest value in the study of this almost neglected material, especially as it is viewed through the helpful perceptions of Analytical Psychology. In the first place, an actual historical person is being studied. One often hears the statement that Christianity is "an historical religion".

This could be construed to mean that the myth is believed to be rooted in a person who was its living founder. However, from my point of view, the "historical" consists in the fact that here one is confronted by a highly developed consciousness in a person living his myth surrounded by many of the great cosmic symbols. It must be emphasized that not only are the archetypes present, but a *life is being lived.* And few things are more impressive than to follow the development of the consciousness of Jesus to its maturation, not out of a desire for *imitatio Christi,* but because of a genuine challenge to find one's own full consciousness. All too frequently even deep analyses can lead to a genuine modification and alteration of personality with but little if any creative involvement of the ego. This should not be the case. To look at the archetypes, to play with them, and yet not to come to grips with them at the level of ego awareness, is to deprive them of their true purposiveness which is to become integrated in actual life.

The second value of such a study lies in its possible answer to those many Christians for whom the symbols are dead or dying. It may also have an answer to many Jews, although I speak only tentatively on this point. The Christian who may find new values is either one to whom the symbol of Christ is sterile and to whom, therefore, "belief" becomes impossible, or one whose experience of life demands a more inclusive God than Christianity has offered. In either case, what originally was the container for spiritual meaning has ceased to be so, and the individual is driven to search for a new inner experience of the reconciliation of the opposites leading to wholeness and peace. To this search, Analytical Psychology offers a splendid assistance, not only through the individuation process of analysis, but also through a consideration of the great impersonal material bearing on this process. The religious-psychological worth of the Synoptic Gospels lies precisely in the fact that they do not suggest "belief" in the Christ as symbol but point directly to the possibility of relationship, inner and outer, to God, and also they suggest that the opposites in God can be reconciled in the individual. And is it just possible that, for the Jewish person, many of the lacks of Christianity do not hold for the Synoptic material and that many of the true values which the Jews have not found in Christianity but which they may need do exist in the Synoptic Gospels? For example, is not the God of Jesus closer to the creative and numinous Jewish concept than the God of later Christianity? Perhaps, also, for both Christian and Jew there is some new potentiality for inwardness and reconciliation. Jesus' relation to Judaism could help bring out the richness of Judaism, and could help demonstrate that he is not just the "good teacher" of liberal Protestant tradition. It may well be that the Synoptic material can serve as a meeting point toward which Christians and Jews must travel, and also as a meeting point for East and West.

The third and most significant reason for attempting to understand the Synoptic Gospels is that the God of Jesus, as contrasted to earlier and later concepts of God, is far more inclusive of the dark and light elements and thus more adequate to the needs of modern man the seeker. May it be that the thrust of God, which seemed to fail with the crucifixion of Jesus, is now, today, ready to become manifest in each individual working to find himself? This God, one might say, needs above all the fumbling, human, imperfect striving that we bring in order that He find a place of birth in us. May it not be that acceptance is necessary, not only of God's dark side and our own, but also of the fullness of God and the fullness of man? In the Aquarian age to come may it not be possible that the teachings of Jesus have something to say about the mutual work of creation between God and man?

SON OF MAN – EXPRESSION OF THE SELF

In an earlier paper entitled "Analytical Psychology and the Synoptic Gospels" I pointed out the following: That the teaching *of* Jesus had been neglected by both theology and Analytical Psychology; that Jesus did not identify himself as Christ or Messiah, meaning Saviour, in either the Christian or Jewish sense of the word; that he did not accept the projection of this on him during his lifetime but maintained a provocative silence whenever asked about it. This non-identification, this neither saying "Yes" or "No" to the central archetypal image, challenges us to specify just what position he did take and what is the implication for each of us. It was also pointed out how richly the meaning of Messiah or Christ, one being the Hebrew word, the other the Greek, is illuminated by Dr. Jung's contribution on an understanding of archetypes, so "the Christ" may be seen as an inner universal image of the Self, which may or may not have been creatively represented in the Christian picture, and which image today is changing and breaking its previous shape.

This present paper concerns itself with the concept of the *Son of man* as used by Jesus, but originating in the Old Testament, and its relation to the Christ image. Whether Jewish or Christian we are not concerned with these things as intellectual ideas but as symbols of living vitality today undergoing transformation. The issue cannot be ignored. New forms must be found for the depths of unconscious images. This paper, I hope, is a modest contribution to that end.

If one were to study the first three Gospels of the New Testament — Matthew, Mark, and Luke — commonly referred to as the Synoptic Gospels, one would be confronted by the term "Son of man" thirty-nine times. One would be impressed by certain facts about the appearance of this phrase. The most striking would be that it is only used by Jesus, or attributed to Jesus, but it is never used about him by anyone else. It is from his lips, or attributed to him. Some of the appearances of the phrase would be in one Gospel only, some in two Gospels, and sometimes it would be in all three Gospels. One might also notice that there was a wide discrepancy in apparent meanings of the phrase "Son of man" and in the features surrounding it — that is, in the descriptive elements. An observation might be made, too, that in some of the instances the phrase came in conjunction with discussion concerning the Messianic issue, the issue of the Christ. Also, it is rather striking that Jesus himself, while he uses the phrase "Son of man", never uses the phrase "Son of God", which is used by others about him. Last — and most important — of the thirty-nine times the phrase "Son of man" appears, fourteen times it is apocalyptic, twelve times definitely not, and thirteen questionable.

Of the thirty-nine times, the twelve times that are *not* apocalyptic are, as far as this presentation is concerned, the historical ones used by Jesus. The fourteen times that are apocalyptic are the non-historical. It may be valuable here to define both "historical" and "apocalyptic". By "historical" I mean those passages or words which probably come from Jesus, versus "non-historical", referring to passages which are later Christian accretions. A typical "apocalyptic" passage found in the Gospels but actually quoted from Daniel, is as follows:

> "And then shall they see the Son of man coming in clouds with great power and glory, and he shall send forth the angels and shall gather together his elect from the four winds, from the uttermost parts of the earth to the uttermost parts of the heaven".

In the twelve historical instances there is no reference to a coming, to sending forth angels to gather together from the four corners of the earth, to clouds of heaven, or to an authority or a judgment, which are the features of "apocalyptic."

The historical-critical basis for a consideration of the non-apocalyptic material is found in the fundamental tenets of New Testament criticism, of which I must say a word. The three Synoptic Gospels are interrelated in the following way — or this is a passible fundamental hypothesis of the relation of documents on which Gospels are based: there is three-Gospel material — material found in all three Gospels, where presumably Matthew and Luke are following Mark (the shorter and generally considered the primary gospel); there is the two-Gospel material — material in Matthew and Luke very closely similar, commonly referred to as Document Q, or divided by some scholars into P and G; and there is one-Gospel material, especially that in Matthew commonly called Document M, and a short document used by Luke called J. There is also editorial addition and later accretion in one or another book. These hypothetical reconstructions form the basis for my discussion of the "Son of man" phrase in the Synoptic Gospels.

If one were to look for the appearance of this same phrase *outside* of the three Synoptic Gospels, one would find it eight times in the Gospel of John (the Fourth Gospel), once in the Book of Acts, twice in the Book of Revelation. These are its only New Testament appearances. In the Old Testament it first appears in Ezekiel, then Daniel, and in the Ethiopic Book of Enoch. The most comprehensive historical account of the background is to be found in *Son of Man in Myth and History*, by Frederick H. Borsch. Thus, "Son of Man" is a phrase which in one sense has a short history — short but dynamic. As Dr. Jung points out in *Answer to Job* it constitutes an "eruption in the unconscious". It appears, comes to its fulfillment, as my thesis will be, in Jesus' own use of it, and then in projected form in one sense it disappears.

Finally if one were to look at the literature written about this phrase in a great amount of research by New Testament scholars, one would be struck by several things. It is generally agreed that few phrases or concepts in the New Testament are as baffling and enigmatic as the phrase "Son of man". One is met by question-mark upon question-mark. Did Jesus use the phrase about himself? Yes, almost surely. On this there is agreement. But how? And what is the relation of the phrase to the idea of

Messiah? Almost all the literature would assume that Jesus used it in its *apocalyptic form* — of which there are fourteen instances — or else that he did not use it at all. To my knowledge very little has ever been done with those vital passages which are non-apocalyptic, or with their possible meaning and value. This is most important to emphasize, because my own hypothesis is that the twelve instances which are not apocalyptic are exactly the ones I consider to be historically sound, to be from Jesus as a description of himself, and to be of great *archetypal* significance.

I shall maintain that the term "Son of man" is related to but is not the same as the archetype of the Self, or to the God-Man archetype. It was used by Jesus to describe the main image which dominated his life and which can be found by others, as it describes in a rather rare way the Self as it operated through him. The "Son of man" phrase describes the Self *at work in concrete life*, a Self lived existentially, not as a hope or a vision; but it is not the same as the Self. We have thus a picture of God coming into man lived as the Son of man by Jesus.

By the help of Analytical Psychology it is possible to grasp the enigmatic meaning of this phrase which is so baffling to theologians who are without knowledge of or ignore the inner world of the archetypes. What is the Self like when it is lived and expressed, when it is brought out of its archetypal, more dramatic, unconscious, or projected aspects? The Self, as suggested, is probably at the root of all Messianic-Christ images, whether internalized or projected. We have extensive research into the Self as it appears in dream fantasy, and myth. We have descriptions of it as it infuses the personality at dynamic moments with its affect and effect with its transforming power. But all too often it is left in a world of its own. To be sure, the Self is in its own world, and yet is it always waiting for manifestation. More descriptions of the level where the eternal and temporal, the conscious and unconscious aspects of the Self are joined in a creative conjunction are desperately needed, in both theology and psychology. And one such description of the movement of the deeper, eternal, numinous world into the level of human existence is shown in these "Son of man" passages.

In *Answer to Job*, Dr. Jung traces the brief but significant appearances of this term in the Old Testament. It appears first of all in Ezekiel (about 592 B.C.), again in Daniel (about 165 B.C.), and in the Ethiopic Enoch book (about 100 B.C.). Briefly, Dr. Jung sees in these three appearances (which are in the form of visions) a "disturbance in the unconscious," representing a fundamental shift in the God-man image, whereby God was becoming closer to man, preparing for the incarnation. God was approaching becoming man, becoming humanized; and man in approaching God was becoming man in a new sense (the divine within) of which the Son would be the offspring. The Self was in formation. A basic change was occurring out of Job's encounter with Yahweh. It is beyond the scope of this paper to dwell on the Old Testament references except as fundamental background. We have here the development in Ezekiel through Daniel, where Son of man is seen as a shift in the God-Man image, as an imminent new reality in the process of "coming", as a birth of a new relationship.

Let me turn somewhat abruptly to the Synoptic record — abruptly and yet in continuity with the Old Testament development. My hypothesis is that Jesus himself historically did use the term "Son of man" about himself, and as a potential in others, but by it he referred to the ego-manifestation and particularization of the Self archetype at his moment of history. It was his way to express the central archetype but not to identify with it or identify the Son of man and the Messiah-Christ image. If, as Jung said, "God wanted to become man" — if God wanted an ego in man — then "Son of man" adds man's ego or consciousness. If the Christ image were the mediating element between God and man, where man could find God and God dwelt in man, then Son of man is the expression of this same element at the human level. It is the Christ "humanized", or humanly expressed yet leaving the Messianic with its own numinosity and unfathomability.

Putting it this way, one can distinguish the ordinary interpretation of the Christian myth from the possible understanding of the values involved in the *Records*' approach, which sees Jesus neither as Christ nor, as liberal Protestantism sees him, as only a "good" man — but as himself struggling with and relating to the deepest archetypes in the human soul.

From this point of view, the picture which Jesus gave as the Individual Way could not yet be lived. Man was not ready. So the image of the Son of man, having been lived concretely by Jesus, assumed again its projected form after his death, when his disciples identified him with it. That is, all the passages in the Gospels which are apocalyptic (and, to me, non-historical) refer to the archetype projected on to Jesus. The Son of man as an Old Testament apocalyptic vision was concretized, humanized, and related to by Jesus. After his death the vision regressed again into archetypal projection.

For Jesus, the Son of man was never in terms of that "which is to come" and to judge. Rather, it is always in terms of vocation, functioning, activity, and inner power. It includes a sense of destiny and fulfillment. In this sense, these Synoptic passages may be opening for us a description of the Self-in-behaviour, existential-incarnation rather than projected potential.

I should like now to discuss the *twelve* situations where this term "Son of man" is used by Jesus as expressive of his own Self-consciousness, of his own internalized relationship to the God-image.

In Mark 2:23-28, the disciples of Jesus are plucking ears of grain on the Sabbath. He is criticized by the Pharisees for the actions of his disciples. In a strategy that is not uncommon to him, he first answers by pointing to precedent in the Pharisees' tradition, namely, what David did when he had need — and then goes on to say,

> "The Sabbath was made for man and not man for the Sabbath, so that the Son of man is Lord even of the Sabbath."

His conclusion is based on the premise that any institution or law is to be seen in relation to its historical genesis, its *raison d'etre*, and that the Sabbath had its origin in man's need. But Jesus does not then conclude, "man" is lord of the Sabbath. No, he says that "Son of man" is lord of the Sabbath. It is not natural primal man, unredeemed unregenerate man, who is able to decide his own needs. For such as these there must be a law; there must be external limits imposed. For the new man only there can be free decisions.

The Son of man, then, is that element within the individual which, if the individual finds it, enables him to make his own decisions. He is able to be above the letter of the law; he is able to act on his own needs, to trust his own centeredness, and to choose. He is in this sense free. He is independent, and yet is related to the law. He is not an anarchist. This is not free license. Son of man becomes the principle of consciousness within the individual, or that aspect of the Self which has about it the moral quality of being able to function through the ego in concrete everyday decisions. Here the man Jesus is acting in relation to outer reality, but what he is acting out of is deep inside himself. This situation exemplifies beautifully the contrast between negative and positive freedom. There are two forms of negative freedom. One is when the person is not free at all because he is completely bound to the letter of the law and to the collective opinion. The other is when he thinks he is free because he does exactly what he pleases whenever he wants to. He is completely on his own to go his own way. For Jesus, Son of man within would be an archetype which would avoid both extremes and give a balance. It would free the person from negative bondage to collectivity; it would free him also from the negative bondage of rebelliousness. There is an alternate reading to this passage in one of the non-canonical records. Jesus, seeing a man working on the Sabbath, says, "Blessed art thous if thou knowest what thou doest." The value lies in consciousness.

It is very striking that at this point Matthew and Luke, both of whom are copying Mark, omit the words, "The

Sabbath was made for man and not man for the Sabbath." They simply have the statement: "The Son of man is Lord of the Sabbath." It is not very difficult to see their reasoning. By omitting the general universal basis, they obviously make Son of man into a Messianic statement where Jesus is reportedly speaking only of himself in his uniqueness. Matthew strengthens this further by adding the statement: "Have ye not read in the Law, how that on the Sabbath day, the priests in the temple profane the Sabbath and are guiltless? But I say unto you, that one greater than the temple is here." This is a striking example of how one can get no picture of the Gospels by reading only one Gospel - their interrelation must be studied to get a picture of the whole.

The second occurrence of the phrase "Son of man" is in Mark 2:1-12, in one of the most radical statements in the Gospels. A man sick of the palsy is brought by his friends to be healed by Jesus. Instead of dealing with the illness, Jesus deals with the almost certain cause in the man as to his suffering. According to the thought of that time, illness was punishment, so Jesus deals directly with the sense of guilt. The radicalism consists in the utter simplicity of his statement: "Son, thy sins are forgiven." He does *not* say, "God forgives you"; nor does he say, "I forgive you." He puts it in the passive voice. He is accused of blasphemy by the Pharisees, who think he is saying, "I forgive you." He answers this by the equally simple and startling statement, "Or is it easier to say, 'Arise, take up thy bed and walk' ", as if these were equated. Forgiveness is redefined here as the affirmation of the margin of freedom, however tiny, whereby a man can move from his bed, from his neurotic determinism, into action. The action stated by Jesus is not sacrifice at the temple for the appeasing of a terrible God, nor is it in terms of a mediator doing it. The sacrifice is inner and personal. Jesus mediates only insofar as he makes the pronouncement, and if this fact is compared with usual Christian pictures the implications are very great. When Jesus sees how his critics are bickering as to his meaning, he goes on to say (after again reiterating the statement whereby forgiveness is defined in terms of responding — taking responsibility), "But that ye may know that the Son of man hath power on earth to forgive sins, I say unto you, arise, take up thy bed and walk."

It is as if Jesus felt that the Son of man in him had this power, but that it was not a unique or messianic power. It is almost as if, in exasperation, he points to that element within out of which his own ability and insight has come. It is a redefinition of the nature of God and a new concept of man. Jesus' position here is as far from the Christian position as it is from the Jewish. His position emerges always as a third one, strikingly and startlingly different. For in essence the only difference between the Jewish and Christian atonement is in the object of the sacrifice — or the subject perhaps. In both cases something outer is sacrificed for healing whether it be an animal sacrifice, or the "blood of Christ who died for our sins". For Jesus, healing came from a personal relationship to a God whose essence is a freedom in the individual, a God who demands only that we use that freedom in a turning toward our deeper sources, in a conversion to Him. Son of man is the expression of the Self making possible forgiveness of sins as an individual internal act whereby the results of sin are not completely determinative, and separation is healed.

The third instance is one of the clearest in relation to our fundamental definition of Son of man. It comes in Matthew 12:31-32, at which point Matthew is parallel to Mark. The situation involves the problem of blasphemy. (There are few words, or concepts behind words, about which people are so vague or confused.) Let me describe the scene: Jesus is accused by the scribes of performing his acts out of power from Beelzebub, the chief devil. Jesus' opponents label the source of his power as black and negative in the strongest possible terms. In characteristic style, Jesus first answers them by showing how ridiculous the charge is because why would Satan want to cast out his own kind. Then he goes on to a more serious and again profoundly psychologically true statement. He says, ". . . all sins are forgiven" but one, and that one is to blaspheme against the Holy Spirit — that is, to know something is right, to be in its presence, and then to damn it and call it black. Jesus could never have replied thus if he assumed the scribes had accused him in the first place only out of ignorance or scepticism. It only makes sense if one takes it that he saw that his accusers did know or sense the source of his power but out of sheer self-defensiveness and jealous manipulation they perverted it and corrupted it. Why does he say this sin "hath never forgiveness"? And is the never, "never" — or "never until"? The terrible damage in this sin apparently resides in the fact that in committing it one is harming the central moral aspect of personality — the power to discriminate. This power is man's blessing and curse. If he uses it, he is indeed above the animals; if he lets it lie unused, he is less than human and a betrayer of himself and God. And this ability to discriminate, to know that there is a difference in values (whatever their specific content is) is the condition *a priori* for the act of forgiveness. Without it there would be no choice. The great thing here is that Jesus was so sure of his own source that he could judge people by their reaction to him. This is a kind of assurance that either is folly or is divine. At this point Matthew, having an account of the same incident, (Mark 3:28-29) and an additional source (Document P), brings in the statement of Jesus that one can say anything one wants against the Son of man and it will be forgiven, but not if it is said against the Holy Spirit. Only the latter accusation is utterly condemnable. The actual words are, "Whosoever shall speak a word against the Son of man, it shall be forgiven him but whosoever shall speak against the Holy Spirit, it shall not be forgiven him."

In this Document P account, Jesus is saying that the Son of man can be criticized and spoken against because Son of man is not to be identified with the divine. But nothing can be said against the Holy Spirit, the center out of which the Son of man speaks or acts. This Jesus knew was divine and not to be questioned. Here, more clearly perhaps than in any passage, the Son of man is seen as the divine in its human manifestation. Because it is *human* it is open to imperfection and to fallibility. Thus, Son of man relates to an inner element which is separate from the Holy Spirit, and yet is akin to the Holy Spirit as it faces towards the human. Son of man is in part the ego related to the divine; it is in part almost the interaction between the two. It is certainly not the ego, but it is also not only the divine. It is the dialogue between the two, within the human frame. Here one sees the two faces of the Self.

The *fourth* and *fifth* passages where Jesus uses the term "Son of man" might be looked at together, as their flavor is similar. In Luke 9:57-58 (Doc. P), a certain man says to him "I will follow you wherever you may go." Jesus answers by saying, "The foxes have holes and the birds of the heaven have their nests, but the Son of man hath not where to lay his head." This is one of three passages where Jesus is warning of perils, difficulties, and obstacles on the way. Here he is stating that if we lived out the Son of man we would live as true wanderers. We would live in the moment — not in the "uprooted" sense, but as the wanderer who lives in the Eternal Now and who does not know where the next moment will take him. He does not have things settled and structured, but is continually in a state of flux and change in a dynamic sense. He is free, and he is secure because he is willing to face his insecurity. It is the natural man who wants to say, I must know what the next moment holds. It is the supranatural man — the man who opens himself to the Son of man image — who is able to say, I do not know what comes next. I do not know where I will lay my head, even though I have many possessions, yes, and a home and all that goes with it.

In Matthew 11:11, 16-19, Jesus is answering the question put to him by John's disciple: "Art thou the Christ, or look we for another?" Jesus gives a stunningly evasive answer followed by a comparison of John the Baptist to himself: "No one born of woman is greater than John, but he does not know the way into the Kingdom of God." (For Jesus, John was a great ethical teacher, but after the experience of the baptism and wilderness, Jesus knew John's values were not enough for entrance into the Kingdom. Yet without John as catlyst there couldn't have been a Jesus.) Jesus contrasts John with himself as Son of man, the contrast being between John as an ascetic, "neither eating nor drinking", and he, having found the

Son of man, who "came eating and drinking, and behold you call him a gluttonous man and wine-bibber." Yet both have been criticized and rejected. So what one does is not important. What is important is the relation of the Son of man to Wisdom (Sophia) from whom actions come, "and Wisdom is justified by her work."

Next, the Son of man as one who serves, who fulfills the Eros function, who expresses service not as a means to fulfillment but as an *outcome* of fulfillment, is beautifully illustrated in Mark 10:43-45 and Luke 22:27. We have here from separate sources two accounts of what appears to be the same theme. It is worth examining because it is intimately involved with a central religious and psychological problem. Is service to or for others a *means* to finding Life, in Jesus' words — or to finding the Self, in our words — or is it an inevitable *outcome* or fruit? For much of the Christian world, to serve has been the Way. One sees a person serving as Jesus did, and one "imitates" this as if it would lead to wholeness, never realizing that serving is an outcome and not a way of wholeness. On the one hand, this has led millions of Christians to do "good works" which somehow never seem quite to emanate the loveliness they ought, either in the doer or in the deed! On the other hand, however, let me quickly add that all too often in analysis the Way to wholeness has not gone deep enough within, or there are blocks that keep the Self from being expressed as service. (Instance: Someone in analysis needed some practical help from friends: his comment: "Oh, I can't ask my friends. They are all in analysis and not interested in helping others.")

What we have here in Mark and Luke is most instructuve. The disciples are arguing about recognition and greatness and who will be first. (In modern language, who has the biggest prestige complex!) Jesus' answer is twofold: If you want to be great in the eyes of the people, serve as a means of attaining this. (Realist, this man!) But if you want to go his way, he asks, "Are you able to drink the cup I drink, and face the baptism I face?" And then he goes on to say (in Luke, who uses one of the two sources), "I am in the midst of you as one who serves." These statements make it clear that ministering service, doing for others, is an expression of finding the Self and not the way to find the Self. This gives us perhaps one of the most real criteria for what the Self really is. There is no such thing — as Dr. Jung once said — as the Self in a vacuum. We, of course, many of us, want to move away from the word "service" because it has such a kind of negative, Christian connotation, but perhaps it is the very nature of the Self that when it is found — when the Son of man is touched — it must express itself somehow in relationship to the real world, and in relationship actually to giving. In Martin Buber's words, the "I-Thou" at the human level surely involves love and giving.

The account used by both Mark and Matthew says the Son of man came to "minister . . . " and adds, "to give his life a ransom for many." This statement of vicarious atonement is found at only one other place in the Gospels, Matthew 26:28, "For this is my blood of the covenant, which is shed for many unto remission of sins." Such a doctrine as this, central for Christian thought, would surely have been much more conspicuous if actually part of the teaching of Jesus. And the fact that at both places there is another account which does not include the atonement makes its historicity unlikely. At no point in his history did Jesus assert himself as a "ransom" or price. But this idea has of course an archetypal basis, and one which he did include in the concept of the individual sacrifice necessary for fulfillment. It was this individual price to be paid which mankind two thousand years ago was not ready for. Is it today? And because mankind was not ready it made Jesus into the new scapegoat. Thus it is not hard to see how the atonement doctrine was attributed to Jesus.

The sixth and seventh situations where Son of man is used are less important but nonetheless valuable. In Luke 11:29-30, Son of man is likened to a prophet and teacher. In two different places in the Gospels, Jesus is asked for a sign as evidence of Messianic power. Once he answers that there shall be the sign that the Son of man shall teach repentance as did Jonah — that prophet then being a manifestation of Son of man in the world. In the Matthew account the reference is to the physical resurrection. Here, incidentally, is an excellent example of the growth of tradition. I think that it is possible that Jesus' only answer to the request for a sign was that there shall be no sign, but I would also entertain the possibility that he certainly could have included in the Matthew account Son of man as the Jonah "preaching" quality. The Son of man has about him a certain sense of vocation, very closely related to Jung's beautiful statement on vocation in *The Integration of Personality*.

> "The achievement of personality means nothing less than the optimum development of the whole individual human being. It is impossible to foresee the endless variety of conditions that have to be fulfilled. A whole lifetime, in all its biological, social, and spiritual aspects, is needed. Personality is the supreme realization of the innate idiosyncrasy of a living being. It is an act of high courage flung in the face of life, the absolute affirmation of all that constitutes the individual, the most successful adaptation to the universal conditions of existence coupled with the greatest possible freedom for self-determination. To educate a man to *this* seems to me no light matter. It is surely the hardest task the modern mind has set itself. And it is dangerous too . . . as dangerous as the bold and hazardous undertaking of nature to let women bear children . . . .
>
> ". . . Just as the great personality acts upon society to liberate, to redeem, to transform, and to heal, so the birth of personality in oneself has a therapeutic effect. It is as if a river that had run to waste in

sluggish side-streams and marshes suddenly found its way back to its proper bed, or as if a stone lying on a germinating seed were lifted away so that the shoot could begin its natural growth."

The Son of man is, then, not only a man who in one sense knows not where to lay his head or what the next moment will bring, but also seen from another angle, he is one whose destiny is absolutely clear and must be followed through in the truly prophetic tradition.

The lesser situation is in Luke 19:1-10, which emphasizes once more the sense of vocation and redemptive action.

Finally, we have three similar instances in Mark 8:31, 9:31, and 10:33 – with Matthew and Luke following Mark. In each of these Son of man passages Jesus refers to himself and his future in terms of the "Son of man suffering many things, being rejected by the elders and chief priests and scribes, and being killed." These passages come towards the end of his brief life – in fact, the first one is just before he starts for Jerusalem with almost sure knowledge of his death.

In these final statements, Son of man again refers to that in the person which takes the individual way, involving conflict with the orthodox and with the collective, suffering rejection by the collective, and a final willingness to meet annihilation. We have here some exceptional clues as to the meaning of what the Self is, as to what it means to pursue the Son of man as expression of the Self. It may not involve for us outer crucifixion in the same way, but it will involve the willingness to go the individual way and to manifest God in reality against all the un-God-like collective elements, so that there must inevitably be terrific conflict, inner and outer. And if one follows it to its fulfillment, it is bound to lead to an even deeper death and rebirth. This is the meaning of being a person committed to the individual Will of God who follows the Son of man to its absolutely ultimate, logical, inevitable conclusion.

To let the Son of man live allows for no deviation — yes, imperfection, certainly — but no deviation from the path which is ahead, even though that path must at all points involve little crosses and perhaps, finally, big crosses. This of course does not mean going out and looking for the cross. It simply means that in many small forms this conflict will come and we must be ready. So that the cross itself as a final symbol for following the Son of man way involves the individual having to take upon himself the pursuit of the opposites, which includes both light and dark, and having to be willing to face the fact that he and God both must suffer, at any moment in which the elements in humanity which are not following God's Will are attempting to do away with it. Perhaps the cross itself becomes God suffering the ultimate outcome of the fact that He has allowed freedom or *is* freedom. If this were not so He could have prevented the Cross, He could have done something about it. But at the very moment at which Jesus, living the Son of man, is on the Cross saying, "My God, My God, why hast thou forsaken me?" he knows that he has taken the power of God on to himself; that is, God in a certain way has lost His power through that power being glorified in man. The cross is the price God and man pay for humanness and for existential incarnation.

The last reference to Son of man is found in Mark 14:41. After the struggle in Gethsemane, in facing his probable arrest, Jesus said to his disciples, "The Son of man is betrayed." A further dimension is added to Son of man when we consider that Jesus had spoken earlier of his impending death as the act of being "perfected" or completed, which implies that betrayal, death, and being completed are related, thus moving the cross from a one-sided notion of perfection to wholeness, making such wholeness part of the Son of man.

In these passages mentioned certain ones are related to the Messianic issue and the Christ image. Nowhere is this more vivid than in Mark 8:31. (One of the great dialogues in the Gospels, this section can be immensely rewarding as active imagination if internalized.) Jesus has asked Peter who other people think he is. Then he asks Peter, "Who say ye that I am?" Peter's clear-cut answer is, "Thou art the Christ." Jesus immediately charges him to tell no one. Why? Is it because he wants to veil it, as many scholars think? Or because he does not think he is the Christ — at least in Peter's sense or definition of it? It is one of the strikingly few places where Jesus does not say a simple Yea or Nay. But he goes on immediately to speak the passage of the Son of man being rejected and killed. Implicitly, yet absolutely clearly, Jesus has renounced the current expectations. Cutting across all orthodoxies, he has almost re-defined the Christ in terms of the vocation of the Son of man being that of wholeness.

Does the Son of man include the masculine and feminine elements? The several passages on vocation and functioning (including the prophetic aspect) are, in all their intensity and passion, masculine thrusts — are direction-serving value-discriminations. They surely come from a man who knows God as will and purpose and choice. On the other hand, the feminine element in some of its facets is evident in such passages as the one on serving — the Eros expression — and the one on flexibility and fluidity, "knowing not where to lay one's head." Are these not from a man who also knows God as protector and as mother? One of the few places where Jesus ever uses the image of "son" without any modification is in the passage about God making the rain and sun to fall impartially on all people — behaviour much closer to archetypal Mother than to archetypal Father. The passage on forgiveness involves both masculine and feminine — the sense of possibility of a new direction being masculine, but this through love, which is the feminine principle.

Why did Jesus use the phrase Son of man at all, instead of the phrase "Son of God," or the simple "I, Jesus"? This is especially important because he knew the apocalyptic meaning. But he did the same thing with the apocalyptic as with the Christ-image — he revitalized it. Why?

Essentially, I believe, he used Son of man because it described in the best available language what he felt about himself — his own self-consciousness. In Christian dogma, one does not have to be concerned with Jesus as a figure separate from the Christ. But *if* one is, one perceives how the use of the phrase "Son of man" represents Jesus' attitude towards himself and his own religious experience, his own achievement of Life existentially incarnate and this possibility for other people. He himself fulfilled the conditions he stated for Self-achievement: the losing of life, the selling all, the transformation from multiplicity to singleness. This process, whenever it may have begun for him, had its fullest expression in the baptism experience where he became a Son of whom God said, "In thee I am well pleased." At this moment Son-ship for him was born. But the interesting question is, why did he then phrase Son-ship as "Son of man" and not "Son of God"? The experience of Son-ship came out of his going deeply into the water and experiencing the "Spirit as a dove." It was the immanent God in a new archetypal manifestation — God wanting a Son and man wanting to be a Son and to have a Son within his own psyche. This Jesus himself experienced. Also, the baptism experience thrust him immediately into the wilderness experience with its questions of Messianic implications. In rejecting the current forms of Messianism, Jesus was synchronously moving with the archetypal development at the human level. Therefore, he was experiencing God coming into man, changing God and man and Son-ship. The phrase "Son of man" best describes this.

Let me turn from the historical to the non-historical passages briefly. There are fourteen times in which the phrase "Son of man" appears in what I would call non-historical passages. It does not seem worthwhile to list them all at this point. All of these statements are attributed to Jesus; none appears apart from him. Many of them, but not all, are direct quotes from the Old Testament, most especially Daniel. Why are they in the Gospels?

Because people could not at that time follow the individual way being prepared by God and manifested in Jesus, the Son of man was not discovered and lived inside. Rather, after Jesus' death and the experience of the disciples of his re-birth in them, they described this experience as the Son of man being alive again. The image of Son of man is recaptured from the Old Testament and then projected on to Jesus as a "second coming", emphasized by the Gospel editors putting all the apocalyptic passages into Jesus' mouth. That is, the archetype of Christ as Son of man, having been consciously lived by Jesus, now falls into the unconscious through projection. And to study the non-historical passages is to study the Christ image in its archetypal, unlived, and projected form. The outstanding characteristics of the Son of man and his activity in these non-historical passages are very interesting compared to the historical use of the phrase by Jesus.

The future is stressed in the idea of the Son's coming, an anticipatory event not yet realized, not yet in time or in consciousness, a movement only sensed, a pre-vision. The time for his coming is never announced; one knows not "when". It will be as a flash. This Son will act as judge with final authority. This judgment he will dispense from "his throne, where he shall sit in glory." The judgment will assume the form of a division of the sheep from the goats. There will be attendant angels who will perform the function of bringing together the elect, the sheep, the chosen. Therefore, in these passages we have a picture of Jesus identified with the Son of Man who is to come as judge, as divider, as cosmic authority with angels. Here we have a continuation in all its features of the Old Testament image which Jung discusses, but *now* identified with Jesus.

We can now ask: What is in common between these passages and the historical ones? And how did the trend seen in the non-historical passages develop? As has been said, the Son of man was emerging in pre-Christian times as a new aspect of an archetypal pattern, a "disturbance" indicating God wanted to become man. This trend is expressed in the whole apocalyptic literature. This was all in the environment of Jesus, and was very much involved with the Messianic issue. In the non-historical passages, the unrealized archetype of the "coming one" has about it a moral quality of judgment, a dividing and discriminating quality. And the integration of elements from all four corners is only possible through the angels. It also has about it a spontaneous-combustion quality, an autonomy, in its sudden and mysterious appearance.

In the historical passages these *very same features* are *recast* by Jesus as attributes of behaviour to be expressed through the personality. They have about them an existential quality, less dramatic than projection but infinitely more real. Dramatic features of numinous experience become very changed when realized and lived. Wholeness as image, and wholeness as achievement, are two quite different stories, as we painfully know.

One continually meets in analysis the difference between the moral quality of judgment and ethic when it comes from a true relation to the center, and the deviation and perversion of it into negative "oughts" and "shoulds" when it is unlived or projected. Dr. Jung has pointed out — especially in *The Transformation Symbolism of the Mass* — that this forms the distinction between the Self-ego relationship and the super-ego of Freud. The super-ego is formed when moral responsibility inherent in the Self is projected into parental and collective images "outside". So the super-ego quality in the apocalyptic passages, the sense of being judged, becomes in the non-apocalyptic passages the Self-ego relation to the creative use of judgment.

Why is all this important? Wherein lies its significance, *impersonally* and *personally*?

The question centers on who or what has come, or who or what of God is available in our psyches for individual manifestation. Who is the inner mediator that can bring together all parts into a whole? Who or what can be the Saviour today, bringing the redemptive element? Where are those to be found in our culture?

For an increasing number of present-day Christians the image of the Christ of the Christian church is not adequate for integration because not total enough, as Dr. Jung repeats over and over again. Even the Christ image that appears in dreams may not be inclusive enough of the opposites in the Self for what is needed, or it may be so autonomous as an archetype that it does not touch the ego. A dream of a woman patient included a Christ-figure, with a real sense of power in the figure. But in interpretation she was aware of two things: that it did not touch the basic neurosis in her unconscious, and that, although she was moved by it, it did not attach itself to or affect the ego adequately. Therefore, the dream image did not contain the Self, which needed to be symbolized in such a way as to include more elements. So many Christians, and certainly many Jews, are looking for a central symbol of God within the Self, even as this patient was.

If we look seriously at the Synoptic *Records* of two thousand years ago, at this link between Judaism and Christianity which is different from either one, we find something of a real prevision for our age, a symbol of mediation that is inclusive and having to do with concrete experience and its fulfillment. We find the man Jesus, with heightened consciousness living a process whereby the Christ-Messianic image was being internalized into the psyche and not projected but not denied. Moreover, he was constantly refuting the projections on to him of this archetype. He was *not* identifying himself with the new self-aspect of God within, as the Gospel of John makes him do, but was using the term "Son of man" to describe the human *expression* of this archetype while not identifying Son of man with the Messianic totally. We find that in Jesus' Son of man image there is an inclusiveness that is much needed today.

The Messiah had come *for* and in Jesus at the moment in the wilderness when he internalized the various images of Messianic hope. This was born out of his baptismal descent into the water, the ascent out of the water, and the descent of the Spirit as dove. For Christianity the Trinity has been the masculine Father, Son, and Holy Ghost. One could say there was in the baptism a Quaternity of Father, Holy Spirit as Dove, Water as the Mother, and the Son. Perhaps the issue for contemporary man is: Which will triumph, the Christian Trinity or the baptismal Quaternity? The latter has very unique features. It is a quaternity which includes the Father as transcendant, the Holy Spirit as immanent, the water as the Mother into which Jesus descends, and the Son who on the divine side is the Father becoming aware of himself, and on the human side is the man Jesus participating in existential Reality. This picture of Jesus as ego related to the numinous is a long distance from the Christian myth of Jesus as Son. The Saviour within, expressed through the God transcendent and immanent as Son of man, is the link between God coming into man, and man with his ego being willing to be spoken to by the Self, to be formed into Son-ship.

The Hassidic statement, "When the moon shall shine as bright as the sun, the Messiah will come," may describe the world's need today. There is a possibility that there are clues in this Synoptic material for a new form of Messianism which would include sun and moon, and would thus encompass totality.

Finally, at a personal level, what is the significance of this material?

In *The Transformation Symbolism of the Mass*, Dr. Jung states: "Christ as the Logos is from all eternity, but in human form he is Son of man . . . as Logos he is the world-creating principle." In alchemy the gold, the *lapis philosophorum*, is described as the "Son of man". In these statements there is confirmation of the Son of man image as an archetype of great significance. But this Synoptic approach to the material of Jesus' experience brings the archetype into a fullness, a manifestation, and a form of consciousness which cannot leave one untouched. It demonstrates the fruits of the Son of man coming within as we see it manifest in one person, Jesus. The Son of man will manifest itself differently for every individual, but there may be some fundamental signposts in the Synoptics, some criteria for knowing whether he has come within us. If we take on ourselves the work of the Son of man we will be working with the expression of the deeper Self archetype and will not be so liable to project it onto Jesus as Christ. We would be living our own myth and depths with the help of the Son manifested in Jesus but not done for us by him.

And what sacrifice does this call for from us? The American poet, May Sarton, has written, "Further limitation releases deeper power." It is far more dramatic, exciting, and alluring to stay in a *participation mystique* with the unconscious archetypes, to "feel" the Christ, have dreams even that move us, and not really be changed. But if we truly relate to and dis-identify from the archetype, living it only in its limited, mortal aspect, we are in process of transformation. This is more painful, requires more consciousness, but it is more solid. This is the meaning of *confronting* the experience of Jesus working consciously with this image of the Son of man. Here the numinous is far more subtle than in its dramatic unconscious form. But the subtlety of it at the level of life really lived, with the sacrifice of its unconscious aspect, is perhaps the demand of history now and is our own and God's deepest need.

INDEX FOR INTERSECTION AND BEYOND

INDEX

INDEX

INDEX

INDEX

INDEX

INDEX

INDEX

INDEX

INDEX

INDEX

INDEX

INDEX

INDEX

INDEX

INDEX

INDEX

INDEX